The
LIGHTHOUSE KEEPER'S
DAUGHTER

The LIGHTHOUSE KEEPER'S DAUGHTER

The Remarkable True Story
of American Heroine Ida Lewis

LENORE SKOMAL

Guilford, Connecticut

To my parents, the late and loving
Irene Homoky Skomal, keeper of our family light,
and the late Bernard J. Skomal, who paid for the oil.
Keep the light on for us wherever you are.

To buy books in quantity for corporate use
or incentives, call **(800) 962-0973**
or e-mail **premiums@GlobePequot.com**.

Project editor: Gregory Hyman
Layout: Mary Ballachino

Library of Congress Cataloging-in-Publication Data is available on file.

ISBN 978-0-7627-5880-7

Printed in the United States of America

10 9 8 7 6 5 4 3 2 1

CONTENTS

ACKNOWLEDGMENTS

Separating fact from fiction has been the yeoman's task in writing this book. I could find virtually no primary sources in Ida's own hand about her life as the keeper of Lime Rock. Ida apparently kept no diaries. No personal letters or correspondences, as far as I could find, have survived in her wake or are readily traceable. It is questionable whether she wrote much during her lifetime. It has been suggested that she might have been functionally illiterate. I doubt this is true, as she was an avid reader of the Bible and had to routinely fill out rudimentary logs and reports in her capacity as lighthouse keeper. It is possible that she was simply not comfortable with a pen.

Secondary and tertiary sources are not the most reliable. In many instances throughout this book, dates have been verified to the best of my ability but sometimes conflict with newspaper accounts, journal articles, and published and unpublished accounts. Ida Lewis did authorize Colonel George Brewerton, a Newport journalist at the time, to write about the first five rescues in which she was involved. The sixty-six-page booklet survives but provides few exact details and is really a recounting of Ida's *memories* of her own rescues, which Brewerton embellished considerably.

Many people were instrumental in what can only be called the detective work behind this book, which has truly been a labor of love.

This book would have had few photos without the generosity of Mark Kellner, manager of the Ida Lewis Yacht Club in Newport, who graciously gave of his time on several occasions and readily contributed the club's personal photo collection of the heroine. This has added to the richness and color of the text. The club's interest in preserving the legacy of Ida Lewis was the fundamental mission of its founding, and the club and its personnel should be applauded for the job they are doing.

James Nolda, senior chief petty officer of the U.S. Coast Guard cutter *Ida Lewis*, was of great help in securing photos and information about his ship. In addition, he connected me with the right sources to help with the historical details about the background of the Lighthouse Service. He even offered me the chance to come on board the *Ida Lewis* and watch the heroine's legacy in action. In October 2001 the Coast Guard also named a training center in Cape May, New Jersey, after Ida.

Let me offer a note of gratitude to the Newport Historical Society, where I retrieved much of my initial information about Ida Lewis. The librarians at New York Public Library in Manhattan deserve special commendation for their eagerness to help and willingness to educate me in the process of research in their vast collection of historic materials. The NYPL is truly a treasure trove of resources. A special thanks to the Bridgeport Public Library, especially librarian Roseanne Mansfield, who worked with me, in vain, to try to find any shred of evidence that would shed some light on the mystery surrounding William H. Wilson, Ida Lewis's husband.

Especially crucial was the verification of the medals Ida received. The more accounts I read, the more confusing the list of medals and honors became. Inaccuracy creates confusion, and I would be remiss not to express my heartfelt thanks to the Orders and Medals Society of America (OMSA), based in Illinois. Because many of the associations that recognized Ida are no longer in existence, enthusiasts and buffs such as OMSA members have provided a true service in lending credibility to this text. The members were eager to share their knowledge and went to considerable lengths to help me. OMSA president Douglas Boyce was instrumental in explaining the differences in medals and in helping me verify several of the medals Ida Lewis was awarded in her lifetime. Jack Boddington, an OMSA member and prolific Canadian writer in his own right, spent hours of his own time helping me find several other awards and medals, photocopying text, and mailing all of it to me, along with books from his own collection. Ron Fischer lent his expertise in giving me background on the Cross of Honor.

The Yachting Museum at Fort Adams houses the original *Rescue*. Several small medals are kept at the Newport Historical Society, along with a pocket Bible belonging to Ida Lewis and the silver filigree teapot given to her by the soldiers at Fort Adams. The Historical Society's museum displays the actual lantern that Ida tended, along with a brief history of the lighthouse keeper. Early correspondence housed at the Ida Lewis Yacht Club indicates that the original founding fathers of the club were in possession of Ida's medals at one point, when they purchased the lighthouse and island from the government.

They apparently handed the items, including the gold U.S. Life Saving Medal, over to the Newport Historical Society in the 1950s or 1960s, according to yacht club member Arthur Dyer. But the society does not have them in its possession.

The staffs at the several branches of the National Archives—in Maryland; Washington, D.C.; and Waltham, Massachusetts—helped with background information about weather, lighthouse logs, and photographs.

Most of the photographs were lent by the Ida Lewis Yacht Club, but others were acquired through the United States Coast Guard Historian's office, the National Archives, the Library of Congress, the Newport Historical Society, and the hard work of my father, Bernard J. Skomal, a fine photographer in his own right.

Finally, a heartfelt thanks to all those close to me who have wished me well on this endeavor and rejoiced along with me in its completion. I am fortunate that they are many. Specifically, I would like to thank my agent, Jackie Meyer of Whimsy Literary Agency, and Erin Turner, editorial director at Globe Pequot, for reviving this amazing woman's story and making this book possible; my son Nate, on whom the sun will always rise and set; my dear family, especially my wayward travel companion, the late Bernie J., and my little sister, stalwart babysitter Aunt Maggie; and cub reporter and researcher Rick Sayers, my husband, who believed in me and this project from the very beginning.

On a final note, for all those who need to write, I believe the world needs to read. Don't stop. Don't forget.

PREFACE

Ida Lewis is an enigma. Considered in her day to be the "bravest woman in America," she has regrettably been lost to history as a mere footnote. Part of the reason for this is that Ida Lewis was not a woman of letters. Although she had been schooled and could read and write, she was not one to journal or keep diaries. If she did, no trace of them is left to us. It is easy to deduce, therefore, that Ida Lewis did not intend to be remembered by history. Or perhaps proper care wasn't given to preserving her memory. After all, she was only a woman.

Although throughout history there are countless examples of those who have sought and achieved fame through their relentless pursuit of it, Ida Lewis cannot be counted among those. Born into a class system that would forever cast her lot in society, she was destined by birth to be nothing more than a common laborer's daughter. Steeped in New England pragmatism, Ida Lewis found no shame in that. Hard work and the simple pleasures it afforded were enough. She accepted that as she conducted her responsibilities as the eldest child living with her infirm father and aging mother at Lime Rock Lighthouse in Narragansett Bay; she tended the light and performed the monotonous tasks that frame the life of a lighthouse keeper. If her life had been the sum total of just that, she most likely would have died a content woman.

Destiny, however, had a different plan. It took her in hand and thrust her into the public limelight without her consent and much against her will. Although she never viewed her heroism as anything special, everyone else did. Ida Lewis rescued people from drowning. She did it well and often, and standing at five feet four inches and weighing 103 pounds, she did so with the physicality of a stalwart man. Word of her rescues circulated quickly and literally overnight, and a country desperate for heroes following the devastating Civil War grabbed hold of her.

But fame is a fickle mistress. Becoming a legend during one's own life can be seductive and create illusions even for the most grounded. Although Ida held true to her Yankee roots, she couldn't help but fall sway to fame's allure. Her story unfolds against the backdrop of the Gilded Age in Newport, Rhode Island, which was fast becoming the vacation spot for both the social elite and the rich robber barons in the 1800s. Though famous beyond any of her wealthy neighbors, including the Vanderbilts and the Astors, Ida Lewis would never be accepted into society. The irony of that is obvious, but sadly, it reduced her to a Newport attraction.

This is a tale of a true and steady woman of the humblest of roots, who as a result of her God-given courage, was catapulted to fame and, consequently, met with some of the most influential figures of nineteenth-century America. I feel particularly honored to be the one who can help this remarkable woman reclaim her rightful place in American history. I hope I have done her life justice.

Chapter 1

PROPELLED TO NOTORIETY

When she performed this duty she had no thought of its being recognized. In fact, I believe if she thought what men would say about it, probably the act never would have been done at all.

—COLONEL THOMAS WENTWORTH HIGGINSON,
SPEAKING OF IDA'S RESCUE

The wintry gale was coming in fast and furious, whipping the water around Lime Rock Lighthouse into a roiling frenzy and sending icy blasts of wind against the house, clattering the windows of the kitchen.

It was March 29, 1869.

Early spring meant an influx of storms into the harbor. They chopped up the still-icy seas and brought spring thaw in with a vengeance. It was 5:00 p.m., and Ida had taken a few minutes to sit in her favorite chair near the hearth before preparing dinner. She was sick with a terrible cold and was trying to collect herself for the night's work ahead. As she soaked her feet in warm water, she heard her mother rustling in another part of the house. Ida Zoradia—known simply as Zoradia so as not to be confused with her namesake daughter—had gone to her room to lie down. She was weary from taking care of her almost completely disabled husband and her other daughter, Hattie, whose lungs were weak and who often suffered through the winter with an infectious cough.

Nagged by the sense that something was amiss, Zoradia couldn't rest. Like her daughter Ida, she was uncomfortable being idle, so she decided to check the lamp's oil supply for the night. She rose from her bed and made her way to the passageway that led to the lantern room, with its window overlooking the water. The view from atop the cramped lantern room was a familiar one, so the smallest change on the horizon was immediately noticeable and called for closer attention. She checked the oil supply and gazed at the harbor and open sea.

Zoradia froze as she peered through the falling snow. There, in the freezing, roiling water, she spied an overturned boat with what appeared to be two men clinging to its hull and yelling for help. In the fury of the sea, the capsized boat was drifting toward Goat Island, moving out of the harbor and into the open channel, which would sweep them into the ocean. And it was moving swiftly in the billowing waves of the stormy sea.

Filled with terror, Zoradia called to her daughter: "Ida, O my God! Ida, run quick! A boat has capsized and men are drowning. Run quick, Ida!"

As soon as Ida heard that men were drowning, she was on her feet and racing toward the door. From his chair, her invalid father frantically tried to dissuade her. He shouted after her that it wasn't her duty to fish the "addled of brain" out of the water. Any sailor who ventured out in a storm knew the danger involved and should expect the worst, he added.

Ida barely heard him. She didn't take the time to put on her button-up boots, hat, overcoat, or even a shawl. She merely grabbed a towel, which she twisted about her neck as she raced toward the boat. Time was of the essence. A matter of seconds could mean the difference between life and death. As she slipped her way across the bone-biting limestones, her feet were cut by the edges of sharp rocks. She yelled back to her younger brother Hosea, known as Hosey, to come help her. He followed closely behind his sister, joining her in the boat as she pushed off from shore.

The hard wind and driving rain battered Ida's back as she pulled the oars with a strength equal to that of a hearty man. At times, it felt as if she alone was pulling the skiff, setting the rhythm of the oars against the overwhelming power of the sea, all the while barking orders at Hosey, who was frantically rowing alongside her. Her strength, both physical and emotional, surpassed his. Ida seemed powered by her sense of duty and her single-minded courage. The sea rose high around them, the icy water pouring over the boat's sides. The snow was wet and driving, hitting them with a fury of tiny spikes. Despite their hard rowing, the boat moved maddeningly slowly toward the deepest end of the harbor near Goat Island.

Ida could hear the desperate cries of the drowning men, a haunting distant din that made her frantic. Desperation was never an emotion that Ida allowed during her rescues, however. This time was no exception, and she caught herself before panic and despair set in. She had to keep rowing, to keep focused on getting to those men, and to block everything else out.

The wind seemed to play with her hearing, and she thought she heard a woman's voice calling. Casting a glance back toward the shore of Lime Rock, Ida saw her mother standing on the precarious edge of the rock's outermost point, wildly waving her arms. She was trying to signal to the panicked drowning men by sending gestures and words of encouragement over the raging gale. They would later tell Zoradia that her cries drew their attention to the lifeboat. Certain that they were facing death, they were close to giving up the fight.

Ida set the oars into the oncoming seas, summoning up a renewed reservoir of strength. She stroked the waves forcefully, conscious that every effort was a battle against time, tide, and an angry storm.

Despite all odds, the small skiff, pitching wildly and taking on water rapidly, reached the drifting, overturned wreck. Ida was exhausted from the brute force that she had to expend just to get the skiff into the middle of the harbor. Her arms were cramping, and her extremities were numb. With the necessary help and strength of Hosey, she managed to pull the screaming men into the boat. The two were soldiers: Sergeant James Adams and Private John McLoughlin, from nearby Fort Adams. They were in bad shape. Rowing back to shore with the men in the boat took double the effort and twice as long. Ida's only concern—over and above her own physical fatigue, pain, and the early stages of hypothermia—was getting them on dry land before one of them died from exposure.

Once on the lighthouse island, Sergeant Adams was barely able to "totter up to their house," according to a newspaper account of the incident. McLoughlin was completely unconscious. He had to be lifted from the boat and hoisted into the house by the combined efforts of Ida and Hosey. It took a long time to revive McLoughlin, and he almost didn't make it. The pair stayed the night at the house, where they were nursed back to reasonably good health.

There had been a third person in the capsized boat: a younger boy, whom the two reckless soldiers had hired to steer. The fourteen-year-old lad had been confident that he could skipper the small boat from the shore to the adjacent peninsula where Fort Adams was situated. With the onset of the storm, it became clear that he was not qualified to captain the boat, which took on water and eventually capsized. Waves crashed continually over the boat, and swallowing gulps of icy saltwater, the boy was unable to hang onto the slippery hull of the overturned skiff. He slipped into the freezing depths of the harbor.

Colonel George Brewerton, who would become Ida's "official" biographer, said of the 1869 event:

> *The boy, if the fault were his, has already paid the penalty with his young life, having gone down to rise no more, till the slow processes of decomposition, shall cause the mutilated corpse to loose its death grip from the treacherous weeds, and drift on shore.*

Ida's other brother, Rudolph, would later recount the night's events as well, recalling: "Sergeant Adams, one of the rescued party, stated when he recovered, 'When I saw the boat approaching and a woman rowing, I thought, *She's only a woman and she will never reach us.* But I soon changed my mind.'"

Ida would later say about the event: "I remember one twilight in 1869. I heard the cries of two men during an awful storm. I put for them in my boat. I could see them clinging to their frail boat. I managed to pull them in, but they were nearly gone when I reached the shore."

It took hours in front of the embers of the hearth for Ida to warm herself thoroughly, calm her chattering teeth, and thaw her itching, frostbitten feet. She was dreadfully ill with a cold, and it would take her some time to fully recuperate. But she still rowed the two men to their base on shore after they recovered.

The last thing going through Ida's mind was fame. Unlike her previous rescues, however, this one would change her life forever.

ॐ

Until that time, she was simply Ida Lewis, daughter of Hosea Lewis, the stricken lighthouse keeper, and Ida Zoradia Lewis. She was one of the four surviving children of the six born of her parents' marriage. She was merely part of the family that lived on Lime Rock and tended to its lighthouse. She was the lighthouse keeper's daughter, like so many other lighthouse keepers' daughters up and down the Atlantic seaboard, who shared in the responsibilities of keeping the light. Ida led a rather mundane existence on the island, helping to tend to the Lime Rock Light, which was situated in the inner part of Narragansett Bay, some 220 yards from the nearest point on shore.

Although other lighthouse keepers' daughters might have been like her in some ways, Ida was definitely not like them. Born and bred in Newport, where she had known no other life than that of a lighthouse keeper's daughter, Ida had no knowledge of how unique she was.

Ida saved people from drowning. She did it often and with great success.

Until that fateful rescue of the soldiers on March 29, 1869, no one but her family and those she pulled out of the waters of Newport Harbor knew of her extraordinary feats rescuing people. A few stories had made the local newspaper in the form of one- or two-line briefs, but none made the headlines. That would soon change.

Overnight, she would become the toast of Newport and even the nation.

∽∾

When Ida risked her life that night in what is considered one of her most dangerous rescues, it was indeed covered in the local paper. This was likely because it drew a response from Fort Adams and was brought to the attention of the customs collector, who was the conduit for much information that made its way off the island of Aquidneck, where Newport is located.

The account of the heroic rescue was so sensational that it was telegrammed to newspapers in New York. Upon reading the account, a *New York Tribune* reporter made the journey from New York to Newport to meet this extraordinary woman.

The resulting article detailed the perilous event in detail—it was Ida's fifth documented rescue, but the first to celebrate her on such a wide scale.

The *Tribune* article also tied Ida's name to Grace Darling's for the first time in print. Grace Darling had become somewhat of a folk hero around the world following a daring sea rescue in the late 1830s off the English coast.

According to reports, Grace Darling, also the daughter of a lighthouse keeper (at Longstone Lighthouse), risked her life during a raging September storm, when she launched a small boat with the very reluctant aid of her father in order to save nine souls from a wrecked steamship. She became an instant hero, and her name became a synonym for an unselfish, heroic woman.

Grace, born on November 24, 1815, in the English village of Bamburgh, was truly the "darling" of early Victorian society. When she was eleven, her father, William Darling, was appointed the keeper of the Longstone Light.

At 4:45 on the morning of September 7, 1838, when she was only twenty-two years old, Grace became aware of a shipwreck during a fierce storm. The paddle steamer SS *Forfarshire*, carrying sixty-three people, had passed the lighthouse when its engines failed. As the ship drifted farther north, the captain hoisted sail and headed south for shelter. Eventually the ship struck a huge rocky shoal and broke in half. The stern broke away, and the fore part of the ship wedged itself on a rock.

Grace reported the wreck to her father, William, but they had to wait until the storm abated somewhat before they could even attempt a rescue. Watching until dawn from her bedroom window in the lighthouse, they saw survivors clinging to the wreckage on top of the rock. Shortly after 7:00 a.m., William and Grace set off in a coble, a twenty-foot rowboat that normally took three men to operate in bad weather, but they could not get directly to the wreck. Instead, they had to go a mile out of the way, around rocks and islands, to skirt the storm.

William eventually got himself onto the rock, leaving Grace alone in the boat. They managed to pick up four men and a woman and get back to the lighthouse only with the extra help of the rescued men. William Darling and two of the rescued men then returned to pick up the last four survivors while Grace stayed at the lighthouse with her mother to look after the first round of survivors. The nine were cared for and fed at the lighthouse until the storm abated two days later, at which time they were taken to the mainland. All the other passengers and crew had drowned.

When news of the rescue broke, Grace became a national heroine overnight, much to her consternation. She was awarded the gold medal of the Humane Society and received £50 from the Treasury. An additional £750 was raised by public subscription for her. Her portrait was painted many times over. William Wordsworth and other poets penned poems about her courageous feat. She had numerous requests for locks of her hair (to the point where she joked that she was going bald). She even received proposals of marriage. In the best tradition of the Victorian theater, the Adelphi Theatre in London proposed (unsuccessfully) to have Grace appear nightly to depict her story onstage.

Grace was a reluctant heroine, much as Ida would prove to be. She tried to hide in the distant northeastern part of England that was her home, denying that she had done anything particularly courageous. Grace died of consumption on October 20, 1842, at the age of twenty-six, the same year that Ida Lewis, the young woman who would become known as America's Grace Darling, was born an ocean away.

Grace Darling was buried in the Bamburgh churchyard in the family tomb, but such was her fame that sailors wanted to be reminded of her as they sailed pasted the Farnes. Consequently, a memorial was erected in the churchyard in sight of the sea.

By the time Ida Lewis was twenty-three years old, she had already surpassed Grace Darling's single heroic act four times over. On the heels of the *Tribune* article of April 15, 1869, *Harper's Weekly* and *Frank Leslie's Illustrated Newspaper* followed suit, sending artists along with their reporters to sketch Ida for engravings for their upcoming editions. The combined circulation of these publications ensured that tens of thousands of people would read about Ida Lewis in just a few days.

She was on her way to becoming a household name.

☙☙

Ida's star reached its zenith a few months later in the middle of summer. It was Saturday, July 4, 1869. The skies over Newport were cloudy, and the air was warm and sticky. But thanks to the breezes coming from the harbor, what would have been a stifling morning in any landlocked place proved nicely tolerable.

To the rest of the country, it was Independence Day, four years after the end of the Civil War. But to Newporters, it was Ida Lewis Day. Ida's name and fame had spread at a surprising speed for the nineteenth century. It was almost ironic that on an island largely inhabited by summer cottagers and the well-to-do, it would be a plain, modest laborer who drew all the attention. With this added local significance, more than the usual number of revelers came out to the waterfront to enjoy the holiday festivities, which included a fine parade and plenty of Ida admirers. Among the concessions were those selling "Ida-wise" paraphernalia. Boys wore hats and ties, while girls donned scarves emblazoned with Ida's name. Girls wore their scarves fichu-style (tied in a knot and off to one side), just as Ida had done in a widely circulated photo taken by Manchester Brothers of Providence.

The etchings of her in *Harper's* and *Leslie's* helped give the world an idea of what this mighty heroine looked like. In truth, Ida was no taller than the average woman of that era, standing five feet four inches tall. She was slim—she weighed a mere 103 pounds. Her size alone made the stories of her rescues even more sensational. Her facial demeanor was pleasant, and her strong features and clear hazel eyes were wide-set and framed by brown hair, which never seemed to gray even as she aged. If she smiled just right, dimples appeared in each cheek. But in every photograph and portrait, she was somber-faced.

More than four thousand people poured onto the streets of Newport that hot Independence Day. All came to hear their homegrown, hometown heroine speak.

They would be sadly disappointed. Unaccustomed and awkward in the role of celebrity, Ida was acutely embarrassed by the attention and far too shy to speak before a large crowd. Even in private, if a conversation began to touch on her rescues, she would redirect it instead toward a discussion about the lighthouse, the harbor, the weather, or her family.

At her core a simple Yankee woman, Ida would never truly feel comfortable with the suffocating attention lavished on her. Over time, though, she came to a point of begrudging acceptance regarding her fame. She felt that her acts of rescue were just part of the job, and no more than anyone else would do in the same circumstance. To her, it was peculiar that society would make such a big deal out of merely doing one's job.

Of her heroic deeds she said, "If there were some people out there who needed help, I would get into my boat and go to them even if I knew I couldn't get back. Wouldn't you?"

So it was on what must have been an overwhelming Independence Day that twenty-seven-year-old Ida mustered up the courage to nervously participate in the day's events, which included a formal presentation of a new lifesaving rowboat, aptly christened the *Rescue*.

The boat was a heavy, long thing: fourteen feet long, twenty-eight inches wide, and sixteen inches deep, constructed of cedar, white oak, and black walnut. The coxswain board was crafted from walnut, with a pure-white finish and gilt stripe all around. All the fastenings were of wrought copper, with not a particle of iron. The cushions were deep red and plush, and the oars—four of them—were a heavy walnut. The cost was estimated to be upward of $250. The boat was paid for by subscription, with a number of dignitaries, including newly elected president Ulysses S. Grant, contributing to its manufacture.

After the handsome boat was paraded through the streets on wheels several times, it stopped at Washington Square. There it was formally presented to Ida by Francis Brindley, former president of the Boston Common Council and a scholar of the classics.

Brindley made the presentation with a flourish:

This boat has none of the glitter and pretense of the silver-oared barge of Cleopatra, which floated on the Cydnus like a burnished throne; but it comes to you rich in artistic skill and treighted [treated] with the kindest wishes of the inhabitants of Newport. On behalf of the donors, and as their honored representative, I commit it to your care, knowing how well and wisely it will be used and managed by the Heroine of Lime Rock, whose name and exploits will be preserved by tradition so long as any portion of the shores of Rhode Island shall be washed by the waters of Narragansett.

Although the historical reference might have been lost on Ida, the attention surely was not. Flustered, she acknowledged the gesture but declined to take center stage. In her stead, Colonel Thomas Wentworth Higginson, a well-known feminist and abolitionist, addressed the throng and accepted the vessel on her behalf:

I am requested by Miss Lewis to return thanks in her name to the donors, and to the citizens of Newport. Miss Lewis desires me to say that she never has made a speech in her life and she doesn't expect to begin now.

She receives the boat with pleasure not alone as an earnest representation of the good feeling of her fellow citizens, but also as a means of doing a little more hereafter, if the occasion should come, in the same direction. She has fortunately learned to do what the proverb recommends as the height of wisdom, to paddle her own canoe. She will endeavor to paddle this one, and if any of you should be so unfortunate as to get into difficulty in the neighborhood of Lime Rock, so long as you can see this boat riding at anchor there, it will say to you as boys sometimes say to a playmate who has fallen, "Come here and I will pick you up." Much has been said about her services in this direction. When she performed this duty she had no thought of its being recognized. In fact, I believe if she thought what men would say about it, probably the act never would have been done at all.

Miss Lewis is grateful to you for your acknowledgment of what seemed to her a simple act of duty; and she is more grateful to Divine Providence which enabled her to do what she hopes never to have to do again.

The rescue of the two soldiers from Fort Adams had been necessitated by their own inebriation, a common occurrence along the waterfront of Newport, where bars and saloons were plentiful. In the mid- to late 1800s, the temperance movement was in full swing and had many followers. As a Christian, Ida eschewed excesses in general and knew firsthand how alcohol had precipitated many of the near-drowning incidents on her watch.

Colonel Higginson continued, making poetic reference to the recurring problem of alcoholism among soldiers and sailors alike, as well as Ida's involvement in the temperance movement:

> *The thought of the dangers that men have undergone in these waters is to her a more serious thing than any praises she has received from helping them. There is many a sailor who has passed the Lime Rock safely, to be ruined by the grog shops of Newport. And when she is aiding in the temperance cause, Miss Lewis is doing a work that will last after the last plank of this boat has been dashed in pieces on the rocks. Or mouldered away on the shore.*

But the presentations weren't over yet. Ida was presented with an elegant yoke made of rosewood with a solid silver mounting, silver sockets, and a crimson cord and tassel. It read:

PRESENTED TO MISS IDA LEWIS
BY THE NARRAGANSETT BOAT CLUB
PROVIDENCE, JULY 1869

"Upon a solitary rock surrounded by the sea is a lone dwelling," began William Sheffield upon presenting the pricey gift. He launched into a flowery, long-winded speech, recounting the heroic event that brought Ida to Newport's attention. "That young girl with resolute purpose and steady nerve pushed her yawl afloat and with practiced arm guided it over the frothing sea to the wreck of a craft which was unable to contend with the elements."

He waxed poetic, obscuring the facts somewhat and neglecting to mention her brother Hosea's role in the rescue. He ended with a flourish:

Her efforts were not for gain. Her high daring was not for sale. The consciousness following upon duty performed was the only reward she sought, and the sweet satisfaction of that poor girl for one short hour as she exulted over the lives she had saved was above the realization of the dreams of ambition by statesmen and warriors, and such as the combined wealth of the Barrings and Rothschilds could not purchase.

Given the heat of the day, coupled with the realization that it would be difficult to top a speech like that, the third presentation was brief. The officers from the steamer *Newport* simply thanked her as they handed her their gift of silk flags to fly on her new vessel.

After copious thanks all around, Higginson bade them farewell on Ida's behalf. The audience gave three cheers for Ida and broke into applause as she stepped into the boat and had her picture taken.

Later that day, a crowd of one thousand assembled across the narrow passageway to Lime Rock. At 3:00 p.m. Ida, dressed in a black gown, stepped into the vessel. It was a far cry from her weather-worn skiff, and the oars felt strangely heavy in her grasp. However, she was well accustomed to rowing, and her new fans watched as she gently slid the oars into the water. Amid cheers and the waving of handkerchiefs, a cannon boomed in her honor as she steered the craft through the crowded harbor.

The shy, uncomfortable Ida had disappeared and another one emerged, filled with confidence and assurance. She struck out with bold, easy strokes, moving the weight of the boat effortlessly through the still surface of the water, as if endowed with the strength of a man. She steered the small rescue vessel toward Lime Rock, around the other sailboats. She then slowly turned to the cheering spectators on shore and smiled as she lifted her arm into the air, waving a small white handkerchief in acknowledgment.

She was at ease now. The day was behind her, she was out of the limelight, and she was going home to her safe, beloved light. But whether she realized it or not, life as she had known it had been forever altered. She was no longer just the lighthouse keeper's daughter. She had become, much against her will, the heroine of Lime Rock.

Chapter 2

IN THE BEGINNING

*Ida knows how to handle a boat. She can hold one to
wind'ard in a gale better than any man I ever saw, wet an
oar, and yes, do it too, when the sea is breaking over her.*

—THOMAS RUDOLPH LEWIS, IDA'S BROTHER

Ida was born of the sea. She loved everything about it. At a
young age, she was drawn to it. It was more than just splashing
in the waves of Newport's waters. She took to swimming early
on and was considered a strong swimmer. Her energy and
strength set her apart from her peers, and it was known that
she could handle a boat with more skill than any boy her age.
A true tomboy, Ida enjoyed being outdoors and spent much
of her time outside. As she grew in size and age, she often
rowed around the harbor for her own pleasure and took time
to help other boaters if they needed it. She was eleven when
her father accepted the appointment of lighthouse keeper, and
she took great pleasure in accompanying him on his sojourns
to the light.

When he took over the responsibilities of lighthouse
keeper, Captain Hosea Lewis rowed the 220 yards from the
Newport shore to the cluster of limestone ledges known as
Lime Rock twice daily. He and his family lived in town, in the
house where Ida was born.

In the 1800s keepers generally were appointed from among the ranks of mariners—men who had knowledge of the sea and the changing weather. They were expected to be able to read cloud formations, wind directions, and changes in tides without sophisticated nautical equipment. They were also expected to give assistance to shipwrecked seamen.

Lime Rock is a cluster of rocks set deep in Newport Harbor—a series of limestone ledges which, before being discovered as a key location for a lighthouse, had been excavated by Newport builders for centuries. As early as 1712, well before Newport became a thriving port, Anthony Young was granted permission to excavate lime from the rocks, according to the records of minutes taken at the quarterly town meeting. Lime was used in the mixing of cement, and the lime from Lime Rock was considered especially durable.

As the harbor flourished and changed, so did the need for navigational aids, including the placement of lighthouses and lightships. In fact, a lightship (in essence a floating lighthouse) had been established in the Narragansett Bay area in the early 1800s. And makeshift beacons were sometimes put along the shore to guide ships and boats safely into port. The beacons were often nothing more than large bonfires or barrels of flammable pitch that helped outline the coastline. They were, however, easily imitated by pirates and other unscrupulous characters who lured unsuspecting or inexperienced navigators to abandoned stretches of beach, where they were looted.

The problem of pirates and looters, as well as smugglers, was widespread, so much so that the Revenue Marine was organized in 1790 to guard against their predations. This service was later called the Revenue Cutter Service—the precursor to the U.S. Coast Guard—for which Hosea Lewis worked as a pilot, captaining his own cutter. In addition, lighthouses were becoming an increasingly important maritime priority.

Until the late 1700s, the United States had only a dozen lighthouses, which were built and maintained by local governments. In 1789, shortly before the Revenue Marine was established, the federal government created the Bureau of Lighthouses. By the turn of the nineteenth century, two dozen lighthouses were in service up and down the Atlantic coast. By the time Lime Rock Light was built, the country had moved into high gear with lighthouse construction. To keep tighter control over the ever-expanding operations, the Lighthouse Board was organized in 1852, and it would supervise lighthouses for the next fifty-eight years. The secretary of the Treasury—who was also president of the Lighthouse Board—was in charge of administering the lighthouses and other navigational aids as well as making appointments. The coast was divided into twelve lighthouse districts, each one assigned to an army or navy inspector. It was this new board that approved the building of the Lime Rock "light-station."

Newport, an island on the southeastern tip of Rhode Island, had originally been established in 1639 by a group of religious refugees from Massachusetts. By colonial times, its location in the Atlantic Ocean made Newport an ideal port for the triangular trade of molasses, rum, and slaves, linking it to Africa and the West Indies. The American Revolution and the embargo during the War of 1812 crippled the economy, although this misfortune proved to be a turning point for the city. Skipped over by the Industrial Revolution, which was feeding the thriving economies of the eastern seaboard, Newport transformed itself into a vacation destination. By the 1840s, decades before the Gilded Age, it was an established summer colony for wealthy New Yorkers. Boston intellectuals, artisans, poets, writers, and thinkers soon followed, attracted by the island's rustic setting and quiet simplicity.

The Civil War introduced a new element to Newport: a strong military presence. The navy moved its naval academy to Newport for four years before moving it out again to Annapolis, Maryland, in 1865. What remained was the Naval War College, which the naval academy moved in the 1880s, and Fort Adams, which would play a crucial role in the years to come for Ida Lewis.

Fort Adams had originally been built in 1799 as an open, irregularly shaped fortification to hold approximately twenty guns. It was situated along Bretton Point, a small peninsula that jutted out and hooked around Newport Harbor, almost pointing to Lime Rock. Named after President John Adams, the fort was part of a series of beefed-up fortifications that were built in the wake of the Revolutionary War, when British troops had easily seized control of Newport. Above the opening gateway was a stone tablet with the following inscription: FORT ADAMS, THE ROCK ON WHICH THE STORM WILL BEAT. While the War of 1812 never hit coastal Rhode Island, and Fort Adams never saw any action, it prompted a wave of concern when the British burned Washington in 1814 (which was possible because of feeble coastal defenses). After his election as fifth president of the United States, James Monroe ordered a second and then a third wave of fortification construction and reconstruction along the coast.

Fort Adams was earmarked for reconstruction, and Congress appropriated $50,000 for the project. Lieutenant Colonel Joseph Totten moved to Newport to supervise it. Considered the premier military architect and engineer of his day, Totten stayed in Newport while the fort was under reconstruction until 1838, when he was appointed Chief of Engineers of the United States Army. According to town meeting records, in 1831 Colonel Totten "took stone from Lime Rock. The U.S. government had to pay twelve cents a cask from the easternmost part of the island but nothing from the westernmost part."

Totten was using the limestone to make cement for the rebuilding of the fortification. The fort was built as a massive work with structural walls constructed of local shale, as well as bricks from clay obtained in Rhode Island and granite shipped by schooner from Maine. Because so much raw material was needed to complete the massive structure, Totten constantly advertised in the *Newport Mercury* for New England contractors who could provide what would end up being millions of locally made bricks.

The magnitude of a fort was determined by the size of the garrison, its length in perimeter, and the strength of artillery. Fort Adams in Newport, though never fully armed or garrisoned and never attacked, was designed to accommodate a peacetime garrison of 200 and a war complement of 2,400 with 468 mounted cannon. Its perimeter stretched to almost

1,800 yards, making the fort one of the largest in the country. Its shape—an irregular pentagon—was considered unusual at the time.

Finally finished in 1857 at a cost of $3 million, Fort Adams was completed the same year that Lime Rock Lighthouse was finished and Hosea Lewis moved his family out into the harbor.

Lime Rock Lighthouse had been commissioned by an act of Congress in 1853, and $1,000 was appropriated to build the crude, stubby stone tower that housed the lantern (which Lewis dubbed the sentry box). A small wooden shanty was built next to it, in case foul weather forced Hosea Lewis to stay on the island. It was completed the next year. Like many of the early lighthouses, the original Lime Rock tower had only a beacon consisting of nothing more than an oil-burning lantern encased in a wooden or iron frame with thick panes of glass. Often, these early beacons had solid wicks and were suspended by iron chains from the top of the lantern. They burned fish or whale oil, which needed to be replenished two or three times a night, and emitted a small light. Lime Rock Lighthouse was built after the introduction of the Fresnel lens, which created a much brighter, more focused beam that could be seen far from the harbor entry.

Work on the lighthouse was not only costly but also hazardous and backbreaking. A crew of laborers was hired to build the stone tower. (One of them was Hosea Lewis's son from his first marriage, Joseph Stockbridge Lewis.) The crew had neither steam nor electric power. They relied on their own physical strength to haul and lift the huge stones, mix the mortar, and carry other building materials and supplies, all of which had to be transported by boat to the small island.

Following the months he was employed helping to build the original light, Joseph Lewis was appointed the first lighthouse keeper, but he left the position after six months. His father, Hosea, had piloted a revenue cutter for twelve years but had been forced to retire early because of his poor health—namely, a bad heart. He gladly took over the position that his son had vacated.

The salary for a lighthouse keeper was $350 annually, and Hosea Lewis accepted the appointment for this sum. The forty-nine-year-old Lewis was appointed on November 5, 1853, and began his twice-a-day trek to the small tower, often bringing with him his constant companion, young Ida, to fill, set, and extinguish the light. Her half-brother Joseph, the previous lighthouse keeper at Lime Rock, left Newport to move to New Bedford, Massachusetts, where he married.

Hosea Lewis was originally from Hingham, Massachusetts. Following the death of his first wife (the mother of Joseph), he married his second wife, Idawalley Zoradia Wiley, on March 17, 1838, in Newport. Zoradia, as she was called, was originally from New Shoreham, Rhode Island, and was the daughter of Dr. A. C. Wiley. Hosea and Zoradia's first child was a boy named Horatio, who died from unknown causes at the age of ten in 1854, one year after his father received the appointment to the Lime Rock Light. Their next child was a daughter, Idawalley Zoradia, her mother's namesake. Known simply as Ida, she was born February 25, 1842. By the time her father took on his new job, she had been taught all the skills that would have been imparted to her older brother had he lived. She quickly mastered the oars and the rudder on their small rowboat and could soon skipper the craft like an expert seaman.

(Misprints in city records sometimes make historical research problematic. Ida's marriage certificate inadvertently omitted the letter *i* from the last syllable of her middle name, spelling her name as "Idawalley Zorada." To underscore this problem with early record keeping, even her mother's death record incorrectly spelled her name as "Ida Doradia," and her parents' marriage certificate gives the mother's name as "Serada.")

As a cutter pilot, Hosea had been hardened by the sea. He was no stranger to the constant possibility of sacrificing his own life to rescue others during the course of duty. It was Hosea who taught Ida how to rescue a drowning man. Countless trips back and forth from the small pier known as Jones Wharf to the lighthouse island were filled with talk of his years on the open ocean as a cutter pilot. It was dangerous, grueling work.

When Hosea was appointed to the position of keeper, the man who appointed him noted that Hosea had proved himself throughout his career and was considered by his superiors to be impeccably honest and above reproach. It was her father who instilled in Ida the seed of heroism. Over the course of their many trips to and from the lighthouse, Ida grew into a seasoned, powerful oarswoman. With time and experience, she developed an innate feel for the boat and composure on the sea. Hosea had already educated her on the fundamentals of taking care of the light, should the need arise.

When he was first appointed as lighthouse keeper, Hosea had to tend the light while living in downtown Newport, on the corner of Spring and Brewer Streets. But the frequent rowing to and from Lime Rock began to take its toll on Hosea's health. For three years he and his family lived in Newport, near the harbor. Several times he suggested to the Lighthouse Board that it would be much more practical for him to live on the island, and eventually the matter was resolved.

In an 1856 report, the Superintendent of Lights wrote: "This is a matter of difficulty during the winter storms and would in some cases be quite impracticable. It seems, on other accounts, that the keeper should live on the spot. That he may do so, a house is necessary, as the present building is but a temporary shanty." In August 1856 Congress allocated another $1,500 to build a "keeper's dwelling." Almost a year later, on June 29, 1857, the Lewis family finally moved into the new home. The *Newport Mercury* reported:

> *One would suppose there was hardly room to swing a cat on the lime rocks and yet a spot large enough has been found for a commodious two-story brick house with ample space in front, and barring that it is a little rough and irregular for a lawn, with a walk leading to the lighthouse and the little beach where the keeper hauls his boat.*

Not only did Hosea have a new home, but the following month his salary was increased to $560 a year. Unfortunately, his good luck was short-lived. Hosea suffered a debilitating stroke in October, just four months after the move to Lime Rock. It rendered him partially paralyzed and completely unable to fulfill his duties as keeper. After several months of convalescence, he recovered enough to walk with the aid of a cane, but he spent much of his time sitting in a chair. More than once, he watched helplessly from a window as his daughter took her life in her hands. He eventually deteriorated to the point that he had to be constantly cared for and even fed by family members.

When Hosea fell ill, his wife and young Ida shared his duties. The brunt of the hard labor fell to the fifteen-year-old Ida. Even though she was a girl, Ida was still a full five years older than her next younger brother, Thomas Rudolph (referred to by the family as Rud). Already finished with formal schooling, Ida put her expert rowing skills to good use, ferrying her three younger siblings to and from shore to attend school each day. Besides Rud, there were her brother Hosea and sister Harriet.

As Ida rowed her siblings to and from the island, her father watched nervously from his chair perched near the kitchen window:

Again and again, have I seen the children from the window as they were returning from school in some heavy blow, when Ida alone was with them, and old sailor that I am, I felt that I would not give a penny for their lives, so furious was the storm—yes sir. I have watched them 'til I could not bear to look any longer, expecting every moment to see them swamped and the crew at the mercy of the waves, and then I have turned away and said to my wife—let me know if they get safe in, for I could not endure to see them perish and realize that we were powerless to save them. And oh you cannot tell the relief when she cried out: they have got safe to the rock, Father. It was a mighty weight off my mind, I can assure you. I have seen Ida in the bitter winter weather obliged to cut off her frozen stockings at the knees.

As is the case with many heroes, Ida's early life helped shape her for her future role. Her family responsibilities and ease in a boat seemed to reinforce Ida's natural inclinations and quick thinking in times of danger. Yet her uncommon perseverance and fearlessness were undoubtedly part of her character, and uniquely her own. Although she was never formally trained in lifesaving—except for some pointers passed on to her by her father—Ida's instincts, Yankee practicality, and coolheadedness would come to her aid again and again in future rescues.

She was obviously the strongest and most dependable member of her family and was well-loved and respected by them. Her brother Rud, also a sailor, often praised his sister's valor and skills. He once said: "Ida knows how to handle a boat. She can hold one to wind'ard in a gale better than any man I ever saw, wet an oar, and yes, do it too, when the sea is breaking over her."

Those skills would soon come into play, in a manner that none of the Lewis family would have been able to predict.

Chapter 3

THE FIRST RESCUE

We have only one life to live, and when our time comes we've got to go; so it doesn't matter how. I never thought of danger when people needed help. At such times you're busy thinking of other things.

—IDA LEWIS

Newport was still decades away from its heyday, the Gilded Age, which was marked by opulence and ostentatious extravagance, as evidenced by the construction of massive estates costing more than Fort Adams itself. The island of Aquidneck had drawn to its shores the wealthy long before the Astors or Vanderbilts graced its streets. Affluent southerners and Caribbean planters came to vacation during the summer months, anxious to leave the oppressive heat and humidity of Dixie and the islands. The expansive white shores and ever-present gentle breezes were a major attraction.

They were followed by Boston Brahmins, as well as a wave of esthetes: artists, writers, poets, and thinkers, all of whom were attracted to the rustic nature of the untouched island and wanted to escape public attention. New Yorkers had discovered Newport, but they had no direct route to travel there easily. Newport also lacked summer housing, so hotels were the primary means of vacationing. Most of Aquidneck was still pastoral, with tracts of land still being parceled in large blocks as farmland. Even if someone wanted to buy a smaller lot and build a summer cottage, few were available.

Real estate development proved to be the key to the boon in Newport in the mid-1800s. Until 1845, land had been used primarily for farming. That changed dramatically under the auspices of Alfred Smith, a man with a vision. He started packaging land for real estate development and, with two other men, bought three hundred acres of farmland bordering downtown Newport. They subdivided the lots and planted trees, and streets were laid out on a grid. Values increased overnight.

Real estate development coincided with the introduction of the first overnight steamship between New York and the island. The ship was part of the Fall River Line under the control of Jim Fisk, an entrepreneur and a controversial businessman. Travel to and from the island became convenient, tourism boomed, and the hotels filled up. To accommodate the crush of new tourists, a six-hundred-bed hotel called Ocean House was built. Eventually, those repeat vacationers became renters and then cottage-builders. Soon wooden summer cottages began to dot the shores, a precursor to the marble giants to come.

Thanks to the same publications that made Ida a household word—*Harper's* and *Leslie's*—Newport was becoming popular, and the world began to view the ocean port as a fine vacation spot. A new "highway"—Bellevue Avenue, which looped the oceanfront and offered sweeping views—was developed. It would soon be home to many of the famous Newport mansions. One of the earliest was Chateau Sur Mer, whose owner was William Shephard Wetmore. His son, George Peabody Wetmore, went on to become a U.S. senator.

Newport was now on its way. But along with the influx of the well-to-do summer visitors were those who lived and worked in Newport. Organizations appealing to Newporters of lineage and breeding—including the Newport Historical Society, Newport Reading Room, and Newport Gaslight Society—began to spring up. Newport had its own aristocracy who would later blend with the multimillionaires from New York society.

On September 4, 1858, Ida had her first brush with this fine Newport stock. She was sixteen, about the same age as the four boys she was about to rescue. The boys came from privileged families, who would have had no reason to meet Ida or her family if it hadn't been for the strange twist of fate that brought them together on that afternoon. Having moved to Lime Rock one year before, Ida had already proved herself to be a capable oarswoman and a fine swimmer, as well as a vigilant observer of the harbor around her.

On an end-of-summer day, four boys of Newport's privileged class would take one last jaunt on a friend's boat and end up being saved by a lowly lighthouse keeper's daughter.

It started out as a simple adventure. Samuel Cambrelang Powell and three of his private school classmates set out in a catboat (a small pleasure sailboat)—the *Hug-'Em-Snug*—to have a picnic on a small rocky island formation known then as "the Dumplings." The island, which was well past Lime Rock, was situated farther out in the wide end of the harbor, closer to Fort Adams. A large stone cylindrical fortress that had been built on the island was used as a shooting target for the nearby fort. After finishing their lunch, the boys again boarded the vessel and sailed out of the mouth of the harbor, joining the other sleek sailboats and pleasure craft that had accumulated on the waves.

As the day drew to a close, they headed back to shore and into the inner harbor. They were soon passing between Lime Rock and Fort Adams, trying to catch the northwesterly wind for which the harbor was known. Clouds had moved in, making it unseasonably cool for early September. Dusk was starting to settle on the water, and darkness was fast approaching. The boys dropped sail and decided to let the tide carry them toward Jones Wharf. The nearly becalmed boat lazily moved toward the harbor.

Ida heard the boys' laughter as they drew past the lighthouse. They started to get a little rowdy, and she looked up, watching the boys wrestle and joke. Perhaps to throw a little adventure into the sail, or maybe to throw a little fear into his fellow classmates, one of them—Theodore Wheaton King (the son of a distinguished Newport physician)—jumped up suddenly. He dashed past Powell, Lance DeJongh (the son of a retired naval lieutenant), and another boy, whose last name was Smith but whose first name is not known. He quickly scrambled to the mast and shimmied to the top. His movement had the expected effect of creating a pitching motion.

As the small boat rocked back and forth, the boys initially didn't seem to grasp the danger of the situation. The rocking made the small boat take on water, and the boys began to shout as they tried to steady it.

But it was too late. The swaying mast and King's weight caused the vessel to capsize. The mast slipped under and the hull turned upward toward the sky. Yelling for help, the boys attempted to cling to the hull of the overturned boat, but there were too many of them. They took turns two at a time hanging onto the cold slippery hull but spent more time treading water.

This was Ida's first recorded rescue. She had been watching the small sailboat move by Lime Rock. When King started his hijinks, she became alarmed, certain the boat would topple over. She raced to her small skiff and rowed swiftly to the four boys, who by this time were gripped with fear. On shore, her father had managed to hobble to the window and used his telescope to watch the rescue.

The hull of the boys' boat was so slippery and small that they were forced to tread water to stay afloat. With temperatures dropping and their clothes weighing them down, two of the boys started to go under, their legs cramping.

Ida finally reached the spot and was quickly able to haul the four in one by one. Her father collapsed into his chair after she managed to get the last one, drenched and shivering, safely into her boat.

"It was my father who showed me how to take people into my boat," explained Ida. "You have to draw them over the stern or they will tip you over. Sometimes they have caught hold of the gunwale, and then I have to make them let go until I can get them around to the stern."

By the time Ida reached Lime Rock with her cargo, Samuel Powell was unconscious. Her mother quickly mixed together molasses toddies and handed out warm blankets to dry off the survivors. Powell was administered stimulants to help him regain consciousness. Once revived, he gushed his appreciation to Ida for her heroic rescue.

But the four were embarrassed by the circumstances surrounding the rescue and feared punishment from their prominent parents, so they never told their families what actually happened. In fact, in at least one family, the incident was never discussed until eleven years later, when Ida was the object of a public love affair. She herself said that she didn't think the matter was worth talking about and never gave it another thought.

A newspaper brief about Ida's first rescue appeared years later in 1898, long after she became famous. Someone noticed a man purchasing an Ida Lewis souvenir spoon, a gift for his wife for their wedding anniversary. When asked why he was buying it, he sheepishly told the society reporter that he had been rescued by her in 1858 and owed his life—and hence his marriage—to her. Whether that man was DeJongh, Smith, or Powell was not recorded.

Within two years of the rescue, King and DeJongh had enlisted in Company F, First Rhode Island Volunteers. During the Civil War, King was mortally wounded at Bull Run, where he was left on the field, only to be found later by his father; he died shortly afterward. DeJongh returned from the war to Rhode Island, where he lived until his death in 1908. Smith, the lad with the unknown first name, died on a battlefield in Tunis. And Samuel Powell outlived Ida, serving as a pallbearer at her funeral in 1911.

For Ida, and the rest of her family, the rescue was forgotten. It would remain that way for more than a decade, when once again fate would intervene.

Chapter 4

THE SUMMER OF 1869

She, who seldom went beyond the limits of her native city, became a citizen of the world—her name, a household treasure because she kept the light shining and feared not the duty perilous.

—Reverend W. C. Geisler, eulogist for Ida Lewis

It was the summer of 1869. Women had finally been given a voice in the political system, albeit a small one, when they were granted the right to vote in the Territory of Wyoming. Although it would take another fifty-one years for the Constitution to be amended to extend that right to all American women, the fight was under way a century before. As a movement, suffragists were as committed as abolitionists before the Civil War. "The only question to be settled now is: Are women persons?" asked Susan B. Anthony rhetorically.

On August 26, 1869, in the very year that Ida was being celebrated for her unparalleled act of bravery, Susan B. Anthony and Elizabeth Cady Stanton founded the National Woman Suffrage Association. And with the country in the throes of admiring Ida, what better place than Newport to host a women's rights convention to "awaken thought among a new class of people."

On August 27, the day after the convention, Stanton, Anthony, and several others set out on the sailboat *Catherine* to finally meet the woman who had matched men on the field of bravery. On that vessel was Colonel Higginson, who had spoken on Ida's behalf at the Fourth of July festivities. In that speech, Higginson, a feminist and an abolitionist, had also made reference to the women's suffrage movement: "She [Ida] has worked out the problem of women's rights in a different manner," the colonel had told the crowd. "She has been accustomed to assuming the right of helping her fellow men without asking any questions."

Ida never drew gender lines about her abilities. In truth, she eschewed any comparison to men in terms of her strength or bravery and was reluctant to become a standard-bearer for the women's rights movement.

Cady recounted the boat ride in the September 2, 1869, issue of *Revolution*, the newspaper she and Anthony published in New York. In the article she glibly took sexist shots at the other male companions on the sailboat, including a practitioner of phrenology who examined Ida's head:

> It is touching to see how easily such gifted men in their hours of ease with songs, anecdotes, wit, and repartee can condescend to commune with those who, according to our state constitutions, are the political equals of idiots, lunatics, and paupers.
>
> The home of Ida Lewis is on a high broken pile of rocks that dazzle the eye in the bright sunlight with their sparkling whiteness. . . . Although our young heroine was busy at the

washtub, she promptly made her appearance, apologizing for her dress. She said she was obliged to work and had so many visitors that she could not always be dressed to receive them.

Just now Ida Lewis is the fashion. No one thinks of visiting Newport without seeing her. In one day she told us she had three hundred calls. She is a frail-looking girl, seemingly with but little force or endurance. She has a marked, pleasant face, light brown hair, hazel eyes, and a chin like Anna Dickinson. . . . We talked of the race between the Harvards and the Oxfords and all spoke hopefully of the time when girls, too, should enter the lists for the prizes of life.

Ida told her visitors about the rescue and of her rowing as a young girl, honing her skills to handle a boat adeptly and to save lives. The article continued:

I rather think those men whose lives she saved were glad to see her out of her sphere that dark eventful day. Imagine those men saved by her skill and magnanimity seated in her quiet home, warmed and fed by her loving charity, safe from danger, fully reinstated in the normal condition of ordinary manhood, holding forth to her on "woman's place," "her inferiority," "her subject condition in nature. . . ." What multitudes of men are strutting up and down the highways of life, pratting of their lordly gifts to reign and rule, who have been fished up from the Stygian pools of ignorance, disease and vice, and their feet placed on solid ground by the heroism and self-sacrifices of woman, who today sneer at the idea of her holding a ballot.

During the meeting, the article noted, one thing was abundantly clear to the visitors: "Ida Lewis is a girl of rare common sense and self-respect. She is modest, unaffected, and seems surprised rather than pleased with the amount of attention she is just now receiving."

Ida handed Anthony and Cady photographs of herself, which she autographed, and saw them to their boat. When the *Catherine* shoved off, Ida breathed a sigh of relief. The meeting had been taxing for her, perhaps because of the women's political nature and their zeal for their cause. Ida later expressed her exasperation regarding the meeting, commenting that she would have rather conducted another rescue than visited with Anthony and her companions.

At this point, it was little wonder that Ida agreed to have Colonel George D. Brewerton, a journalist, write what she would endorse as the official accounting of her life to date. Perhaps she was getting tired of repeating it herself. The clamor for information and for "everything Ida" had become oppressive. The small sixty-six-page book, *Ida Lewis, The Heroine of Lime Rock*, was published in October 1869 in the wake of the public furor over Ida. In its flyleaf, she testifies to its accuracy, but throughout, Brewerton asserts that even Ida had a hard time recalling the dates of the previous rescues and rarely remembered the names of those she had saved or followed up on what later happened to them. Ida wrote:

> *His [Brewerton's] account of the Rescues and other matters connected with my history and parentage are truly told, the particulars having been furnished by myself. I commend this*

*book to those who may be curious to know more of my life
and antecedents, as a faithful record and the only one I have
authorized to be given.*

Perhaps Ida felt the pamphlet would make her life easier
in dealing with the relentless public interest in her rescues,
especially since she had also become the recipient of several
influential humanitarian awards that spring following the
most recent rescue. It must have come as a shock to her when
she opened a letter from the Life Saving Benevolent Association of New York. In it, she found a check for $100 and a
package containing a Moroccan red, velvet-lined case. Lifting
the heavy silver medal out of the handsome case, Ida read
the inscription: "Presented to Miss Ida Lewis as a testimo-
nial to her skill, courage, and humanity in rescuing two men
from drowning in the harbor of Newport, R.I. during a severe
storm on the 29th of March."

Ida obviously knew where New York was, as the inspector for the Third Lighthouse District (to whom she reported)
was located on Staten Island. But she had never been there,
although she would come close when she married the next
year.

The Life Saving Benevolent Association of New York was
founded in 1848 by a group of prominent merchants, ship-
owners, and underwriters who realized the need to establish
a system for saving lives. The loss of lives was tragic but also
costly, especially to shipping company owners and insurance
companies underwriting the ventures. Thus was born the Life
Saving Benevolent Association of New York, which in part

created a reward system to encourage lifesaving along the eastern coast near New Jersey and Long Island, New York.

The organization asked for and received from Congress and the secretary of the Treasury a $10,000 appropriation. Its mission was

> to recognize and reward courage, skill, and seamanship displayed in the rescue of human life on the sea or any navigable waters . . . and to award medals, medal pins, and sums of money for life saving, to encourage training in seamanship, lifeboat work, methods of rescue in the water, and the resuscitation of victims of submersions, and to perform such other services of benevolence.

Ida never applied for the award, or even knew that she was being considered. The impact of receiving her first medal and what was then a sizable sum of money must have been overwhelming. It set the tone for the rest of the summer. Accolades kept coming.

Several weeks later, at the end of May 1869, the Rhode Island General Assembly passed a resolution honoring Ida Lewis, the first such governmental recognition for this lighthouse keeper's daughter. In a document accompanying the ornate parchment resolution, John Bartlett, the secretary of state of Rhode Island, expressed the state's gratitude to the twenty-seven-year-old: "I take pleasure in transmitting to you a resolution unanimously adopted by the General Assembly of this state at its late session in Newport acknowledging your valuable services in saving so many lives from drowning."

The document, complete with gold seal, read:

Resolved: That this General Assembly desires to recognize officially the heroism of Miss Ida Lewis, of Newport, in repeatedly saving the lives of drowning men, at the risk of her own and we are proud that one of our own citizens, by her courage and humanity, has won admiration of the whole country.

Less than two weeks later, another honor arrived. Major General Henry Hunt, the commanding officer of the Fifth Regiment U.S. Artillery and the Garrison of Fort Adams, sent a letter thanking Ida for rescuing Sergeant Adams and Private McLoughlin. Included with the note was $218, contributed by the garrison's thankful officers and soldiers. The garrison also presented her with a gold watch.

After a whirlwind two months of newspaper publicity, the world finally woke up to the existence of this heroine. Newport dedicated Independence Day to her. Ida was reeling. Given the times, it was a weighty matter for the town of Newport to dedicate that day in her honor. The Civil War had ended a mere four years earlier. Wounds had yet to heal, but parts of the country were still riding high on a euphoric sense of patriotism; a surge of nationalism was spreading through the eastern states. When July 4 rolled around, Ida was quite reluctant to be the center of attention, but she obliged out of a sense of duty.

After receiving the beautiful new rowboat *Rescue,* Ida had nowhere to house it. Her own skiff was tied to a mooring on the edge of Lime Rock. The situation was rectified the next day. Among her steady stream of visitors during that summer was U.S. Customs Collector Seth Macy, a powerful man of the day, for Newport was a customs port, and the collector's position—a political appointment—enjoyed a lofty status.

At that time, the nation was divided into customs collection districts. Each district had a headquarters port with a customhouse and usually subports as well. When initially set up, the Customs Collection District of Newport, Rhode Island, consisted of Newport as the headquarters port and North Kingston, East Greenwich, Barrington, Warren, Bristol, and Westerly as ports of delivery. Some of the ports of delivery later became customs districts themselves. (In 1801 Bristol and Warren became a separate collection district, and in 1842 Westerly and Stonington, Connecticut, were joined and became a separate district.)

The Collector of Customs was the chief officer of the district and was responsible for numerous tasks. Not only did he collect duties, keep records, and report financial transactions to the secretary of the Treasury, but he was also responsible for enforcing the revenue laws and for collecting fines and penalties for violation of those laws. In addition, he was responsible for documenting American merchant vessels, recording the entrances and clearances of vessels within the district, and administering the customhouse. Moreover, he was accountable for the lighthouses within his district and for the protection of American seamen and passengers on American vessels, as well as the revenue cutters within his district.

The Collectors of Customs were extremely influential federal officials. For most of the nineteenth century, the customs service was the largest civil agency in the federal government. The collectors appointed and were in charge of the deputy collectors, surveyors, inspectors, weighers, gaugers, and other customs employees within their districts. This political patronage enhanced a collector's power. It was through Macy that much of the information about Ida's rescues was filtered to key figures in the government.

Accompanying Collector Macy on that day after Independence Day were two highly controversial, very wealthy businessmen: Jim Fisk and Jay Gould.

Fisk was the president of the Fall River Steamship Company, which was instrumental to the tourism boom. Gould had already gained a reputation as an unscrupulous businessman. Both of them were looked upon with great disdain, especially by the Vanderbilts, their archrivals. In the world of robber barons, there were the captains of industry, such as Vanderbilt, Carnegie, and Rockefeller, and then there were Jim Fisk and Jay Gould, who lacked any conscience and preyed on weak businesses to develop their own empires.

But some say that Fisk and Gould had another side, which could be glimpsed on that July day in 1869. Upon stepping onto the island, Fisk noted that Ida had nowhere to house the glorious boat, so he ordered Macy to have a boathouse constructed at his own expense. He also had a silk pennant made for the *Rescue*, which Ida had framed and placed on the wall of her home. Jay Gould presented her with lavish gold oarlocks for the boat. However, the notorious twosome's true nature showed itself just two months later, when they would attempt to control the U.S. gold market.

Meeting Fisk and Gould, as well as a host of other wealthy, powerful, high-profile figures of the day, added a new dimension to Ida's celebrity. Her instant fame was perhaps the hardest thing for Ida to grasp at this point, being generally uncomfortable with the attention. But to become the center of attention—to be instantly admired by those who existed at the very top of the class system in the late 1800s—was quite a different story. Ida may not have realized the importance of this attention.

Although she might not have ever heard of the Sorosis Society, in July 1869 she was made an honorary member of the elitist women's group and was sent a gold engraved pin from the New York Chapter. Modeled after male secret societies such as the Masons, the Sorosis Society was the premier women's group of the eighteenth century. Its primary function was as a literary group, even though it had the trappings of a volunteer organization.

Being made a member, honorary or otherwise, was most likely lost on Ida, who, even if she had had the inclination and desire to read novels, had little time to do so. But Ida knew the importance of that pin. Later photographs and events often showed her wearing it clasped at her neck or on her shoulder.

Ida made no pretense of culture. She was not educated in any formal sense; her schooling ended at age fifteen when she and her family relocated to the island. Ida was not refined. She had traveled no farther than the city limits of Newport, unless one defines the harbor as being outside the city. Her life was very limited, and her understanding of society etiquette nonexistent.

But she would never have the chance to embarrass herself. That summer of 1869 was replete with throngs of visitors. As Ida herself said, "Every Mrs. Astor and every Mrs. Vanderbilt and every Mrs. Belmont you ever heard of called on me with whole boatloads of men and women that all talked to me at once and treated me as if I were a kind of real queen."

But despite all the attention she received from the upper classes, she would never once be included on a guest list to any lavish affair. Not once did Ida have a glimpse of the inside of any of the oversized summer cottages or outrageous mansions. She was, at most, an attraction.

If Ida needed some time to deal with her own popularity, she wasn't afforded the luxury. That summer of 1869 alone, her father counted between nine thousand and ten thousand visitors who made the pilgrimage to Lime Rock to meet the heroine. On a given day, she was fond of telling reporters, she would shake upwards of six hundred hands.

Some of the visitors were quite prestigious. Her most important one was undoubtedly Ulysses S. Grant. Inaugurated the eighteenth president just months before, Grant was visiting Newport and requested an interview with Ida. His schedule was overbooked, so he asked Ida (through correspondence) if she could row to shore and meet his entourage, which included his wife.

As always, she obeyed. A nervous Ida, dressed in her holiday attire, used *Rescue* to row over to the meeting place at the end of Long Wharf. She seldom used the new boat, as she instead preferred her old skiff, called *Courageous Child of Columbia*. She was brought to the carriage where Grant was waiting. The meeting was brief, but Grant expressed his great pleasure at meeting a lady so distinguished in the field of humanity. He told her, "I am happy to meet you, Miss Lewis, as one of the heroic, noble women of the age."

By some reports, Grant was so insistent on meeting Ida that he supposedly said, "I have come to see Ida Lewis, and to see her I'd get wet up to my armpits if necessary." When asked what he did say to her, Ida shrugged it off, as all flattering speeches sounded alike to her.

Other names tied with that summer and the subsequent ones included General William Tecumseh Sherman and Admiral George Dewey, who would visit often during his appointment as secretary of the Lighthouse Board. On his first trip to Lime Rock, he told Ida, "Miss Lewis, I want to smoke on your half-acre rock for a half-hour." They spent many afternoons chatting easily while he smoked. When General Sherman arrived, he sat on the rock for "nearly an hour, asking me questions about my life and saying he was glad to get to such a peaceful place," Ida said.

As she herself would note, "There's hardly a great admiral or noted general that hasn't been here to see me." Perhaps men of celebrated bravery found in Ida what they found in themselves: the ability to act in the face of danger and great peril to one's own safety.

She was particularly pleased with the comments of Secretary of the Treasury George S. Boutwell (who served from 1869 to 1873). He came that summer to meet her, and she delighted in telling the story of their encounter: "He said he came purposely to thank me personally for saving the life of a soldier from Fort Adams because the light was in his department, and he was proud to have a woman in his department who was not finicky about getting her hair wet."

But not all the visitors were famous. In fact, of the thousands of admirers who supposedly came to meet her, only a few were. And they weren't always polite, either. A *Boston Journal* article that was published the following summer recounted the months following Ida's catapult to fame:

> *Everybody thought Ida Lewis would be left in peace this season after the furor of last, the public soon tiring usually of such demonstrations but such is not likely to be the case. The rush of visitors has commenced again, and Lime Rock is one of the greatest attractions to strangers. It is estimated that over 10,000 persons called upon Miss Lewis last summer. According to newspaper accounts, Mr. Lewis actually counted over 9,000 tourists to the island and remarked that there were probably not twenty who compensated her for the trouble they gave. Her time was fully given to visitors and in consequence, she had to have her own work done. People would land on the rock, prowl over the house, quiz the family, pry into household affairs, patronizingly ask the age of each person and what they lived on and how they felt when Ida was saving souls.*

Many of them were downright rude, taking photographs, newspaper clippings, and memorabilia that she had neatly tucked away and willingly shown them. Countless times she was told that they would be returned, so they were lent out, never to be seen again. Throughout her life, pranksters would mock her by pretending to need her help, yelling out "Ida, Ida, come save me," and then break into peals of laughter when she took the call seriously. Many visitors expected her to pick them up on shore and row them to her home. Others would want her to stop her chores to visit with them. Initially she complied, but she ceased the practice as she got older, realizing that her work would not get done.

With the onslaught of visitors came a glut of attention. She became a popular figure for painters and photographers. The new craze at the time was color postcards, and many were made of her. Brewerton, her biographer, executed a fifty- by thirty-three-inch oil painting of Ida, depicting her bareheaded and rowing in an angry sea to save those hanging off a capsized boat.

Offers came in for her to see the world, including one as part of a traveling vaudeville act that would have paid her $1,500. Two musical pieces were published with her name in the title: the "Ida Lewis Mazurka," which followed a Polish folk song format, and the "Ida Lewis Waltz." Multiple poems appeared. Some were published; others were just penned and sent to her.

She was inundated with fan mail, as well as a few bizarre, or at least unusual, letters. She was especially touched by those who wanted to help her family. Reading that her father, Hosea, was stricken with paralysis following a stroke, some people sent recipes and ingredients (including oatmeal and maple syrup) for hasty pudding. Others sent money and clothing. Many letters contained requests for photos and autographs, even locks of hair.

But by and large, the bulk of the letters came from men offering one thing: matrimony. Apparently men were mad for Ida, even if they hadn't met her. Some suitors sent photos of themselves. One fellow from West Point sent his father to meet her; the father brought along his son's picture and the name of the hometown mayor as a personal character reference. He told Ida that she might learn to love his son. Taken aback, Ida responded that the son was too young, merely an adolescent.

That same summer of 1869, Grant's vice president, Schuyler Colfax, made a sojourn to meet the new heroine. His visit was rather extended, perhaps because his own cousin was a lighthouse keeper and he felt a kindred spirit to Ida.

Harriet Colfax was the second keeper of Michigan City Light, which she took over in 1861. Her appointment was most likely arranged by her cousin, then a congressman. Formerly a schoolteacher, she moved with her brother to the city to start a newspaper and work as a typesetter for him. When her brother left town because of frail health, she stayed on and took up the position as keeper. Michigan City Light was quite different from Lime Rock. Harriet was expected to walk the long length of an elevated pier that spanned some 1,500 feet across Lake Michigan, at the end of which was a beacon to be maintained. Rough waves and high winds lashed across the planks of wood, presenting a real danger in crossing.

Harriet's log documented the weather, storms, and damages done to the light and pier, recounting the vicious weather of the lake and the constant barrage of winter gales and blinding rainstorms. If Ida had written detailed logs, they most likely would have been filled with short, objective entries, blandly detailing supplies and the tasks of tending the light.

Harriet's log and those of other lighthouse keepers were sparse in their detailing but did offer a glimpse into their lives. In rare descriptions, Harriet spoke of watching the fantastic color play of the Northern Lights and the silent eclipse of the moon. She wrote about listening to the ricocheting hail off the roof of the house and pondered the beauty of a double rainbow. Unlike Ida, she had no callers of note, except for her visits from the lighthouse inspector. She was not remembered for having saved anyone with her stalwart strength. Like Ida, however, she was a small woman, and some considered her frail. She served as keeper until 1904, when she retired. She died soon after at the age of eighty.

It is likely that Schuyler Colfax spoke of his cousin Harriet during his visit to Lime Rock that day. He arrived on the island uninvited and rather abruptly. He was accompanied by his new bride, Ellen Wade, as well as General Hunt (the commander of Fort Adams) and several other officers. Ida was lying down, resting in her room, most likely trying to escape from the visitors. Her mother greeted Colfax, who asked that she not reveal his identity to Ida. He wanted to meet her in her everyday clothes, without any special effort.

Ida came out, wiping sleep from her eyes, and was taken by surprise. Apparently the visit was cordial. At the end of their long stay, Ida walked the distinguished visitors to the docked barge, and Colfax turned to her.

He asked her if she was engaged.

Ida was indeed engaged. In fact, she had been engaged for three years to a captain of a yacht from Black Rock Harbor in Bridgeport, Connecticut. Although Colfax fell short of dissuading her to marry, he did say that if she married, she would become a Mrs. Somebody rather than Miss Ida Lewis. And more than likely, she would be forgotten. He added that she would be sensible to retain her maiden name, like many distinguished women in the public eye.

Ida's eyes flashed when she retorted: "If I should ever marry, no hope of personal gain will ever make me a party to even a conventional deceit. When I get a husband I will bear his name and no other, let the world forget me as it will."

Despite the endless stream of marriage proposals from unknown, unseen suitors, Ida chose to marry the captain, whom she had met during the three summers that his yacht was docked near Lime Rock.

His name was William Heard Wilson, and he pressed Ida to marry him, particularly since her name had drawn so much public attention. His family hailed from Fairfield, Connecticut, the town next to Bridgeport. Like Ida, he was twenty-eight years old. On their marriage certificate, his occupation is listed as "seaman." Ida's is listed as "none."

On October 23, 1870, a year after Colfax's visit, they married in Newport at the Methodist Episcopalian Church on Thames Street. Ida's funeral would be held forty-one years later in that same church.

Ida's wedding was most likely a private affair and one that she would have fought to keep simple and discreet. Following her marriage to the captain, Ida made what would be the second biggest mistake of her life, following just on the heels of her first.

She left Lime Rock for the bustling harbor of Black Rock, Connecticut.

There she found a much different life than she had known in Newport. Newport Harbor had experienced its heyday in the 1700s, with the port establishing itself during the triangular trade among the West Indies, Africa, and America. The 1800s were less prosperous, with the island never taking part in the highly profitable whaling industry, which spurred the economies of much of the eastern seaboard. Black Rock, on the other hand, rivaled much larger seaports in its level of activity. Hundreds of clippers and schooners frequented the waterways daily.

Bridgeport's shoreline, although an active vacation destination in the late 1800s, did not attract the caliber of wealthy visitors that Newport did. It was crowded, with a developed seafront. The winters were much harsher than Ida was used to, and the people were of a different sort. New Englanders in Connecticut seemed less friendly, and it was not easy to establish friendships. Ida knew no one, except her husband and new in-laws. She was not a naturally outgoing person. She quickly withered without the comfort of her surroundings and those who bolstered her spirit.

They settled in Black Rock, close to William's father, Wakeman Wilson, who owned a large plot near a point overlooking the harbor. Even though Ida's notoriety should have followed her, no one seemed to take much notice of her arrival. She was more of a curiosity than anything else.

Unlike Newport, people by the hundreds didn't stop by to visit her, and if they did, she hadn't much to show them. There was no lantern to display, no tour to give of the white, shiny island, no overturned boats to row out to, and no lives to save. Most likely she didn't even have a boat to ply her skills. Ida had nothing to do but keep house for her some-time husband, a seafaring yachtsman who was away more than he was home.

Perhaps as she glanced out toward the open sea outside the harbor, she looked desperately in the direction of Lime Rock, searching for some familiar view. Instead, she likely had the view of another lighthouse. Fayerweather Island jutted out into the opening of the harbor; it consisted of a skinny slip of rocks covered with stubbly brush. On it was a tall whitewashed brick lighthouse, with an adjacent small wooden home. In it was another female lighthouse keeper—the keeper of the Black Rock Light.

Born in 1795, Kate Moore was seventy-five when Ida, then twenty-eight, moved to Bridgeport after her marriage in 1870. It was the year before Kate's own disabled father, for whom she faithfully kept the wick, would finally die. Kate had cared for him, receiving nothing in the way of recognition or recompense from the federal government.

To keep the light of Fayerweather Island burning, Kate had to sleep facing the tower. "I slept at home, dressed in a suit of boy's clothes, my lighted lantern hanging at my headboard and my face turned so that I could see shining on the wall the light from the tower and know if anything had happened."

And if it did, it was Kate, not her father, who had to tend it. As Kate recounted, "Our house was forty rods from the lighthouse, and to reach it I had to walk across two planks under which on stormy nights were four feet of water. And it was not too easy to stay on those slippery wet boards with the whirling and the spray blinding me."

Fayerweather was a skinny island that hooked into the entrance of Black Rock Harbor. It could be reached only by rowboat.

Storms were quite commonplace on Fayerweather Island, as they were in Newport. But the winds were fierce enough in 1821 to completely level the lighthouse. It was rebuilt, and the light kept burning under her vigilance. Kate built her life around her time on the island. Like most lighthouse keepers, she raised animals, took care of a garden, and found other ways to make money. She tended oyster beds and carved wooden decoy ducks to sell (today they are considered collector's items).

When Kate's father passed away in 1871 at the age of ninety-eight, she took drastic measures to ensure that she would finally be compensated for her hard work of fifty-plus years. Concerned that the government might send a replacement, she holed up in the house with her father's body for a week until her own appointment came through.

Her fear was not unfounded. It was commonplace in the early years of the Lighthouse Board for keeper appointments to be made by the president or by the secretary of the Treasury. It was common for the position to be a reward for political patronage. Often, the position went to men with no seafaring experience. All the new appointee needed to do was to show up with his slip of employment at the lighthouse, and the current keeper would be expected to vacate the property immediately.

If anyone would understand Ida, it was Kate. Kate also was a heroine. She knew what it was like to save lives and to haul her small rowboat out into the rolling waves in the growling face of a fierce storm. In the history of lighthouse keepers, Kate has more documented rescues attributed to her than Ida. She saved at least twenty-three souls from the ravaging grip of the sea. She pulled half-drowned seamen from sinking wrecks in perilous storms. She risked her own life on many occasions. She had to spend countless hours with the dead bodies of sailors who had washed ashore, as she waited for the government to gather them for proper burial.

But unlike Ida, Kate was ignored. Except in the twilight of her life, no newspaper reporters, society matrons, or balladeers thronged to Fayerweather to get a glimpse of the heroine there. Putting her life in harm's way was never rewarded with even a faint glimmer of the limelight. She lived an isolated life, collecting $350 a year and taking care of business.

When Kate left the light, she did so without ever looking back. She retired in 1878 at eighty-three. But longevity clearly ran in the family, as she lived another twenty-two years, dying at 105. Her life at Fayerweather was bittersweet. When asked if she missed the lighthouse life, she was matter-of-fact: "Never. The sea is a treacherous friend." Yet she lived out the rest of her life in a small house on the shore, within clear view of the lighthouse she had called home.

Unlike Kate, Ida desperately missed her home. She was miserable in her married life in this strange place. For without Lime Rock, without her light, she was nothing.

The marriage proved to be a disaster—in fact, so much so that she refused to speak of it, at least in public or to the media, for the remainder of her life. According to published articles from later in her life, Ida became a devout, church-going Christian. Although she openly supported separation when a mistake had occurred, she was deeply entrenched in the belief that divorce was a sin.

"What God has joined together let no man put asunder," was the mantra Ida often repeated when discussing the sanctity of matrimony. When she died, her brother Rud told reporters, "My sister and her husband could not live happily together. So they soon parted."

In less than two years, she left Wilson back in Bridgeport. He never once visited her for the remainder of her life, and they never divorced. She kept her legal name for a while but eventually reverted back to her maiden name. It suited her better and made Vice President Colfax's words prophetic.

Not much, if anything, is known about Ida's marriage to Wilson. Some speculated that Wilson had a drinking problem, which was not uncommon with seafaring men of the day. Given Ida's dedication to the temperance movement, it would have been a bone of contention between the two and not easily resolved. Other reports speculated that Wilson had actually died. This, however, was probably untrue, as Ida never confirmed such reports in any newspaper interviews in the years following their breakup. Apparently, he was alive but not in contact with her. Neither one of them tried to visit or write to the other. According to at least one account, Wilson had a depressive or manic personality and was difficult to live with and prone to dark moods.

Whatever the case, given Ida's strong sense of duty and commitment to following Christian dogma, their marital problems must have been substantial for her to have left him. The fact that she would never speak of the union was testimony to that.

A little more than two years after her marriage, perhaps prompted by her father's death on November 17, 1872, Ida Lewis was back at her home on Lime Rock.

Chapter 5

KEEPING THE WICK

> As the light that she kept so faithfully was a beacon to
> the mariner within the circle of its reach, so the light of
> her brave unselfish spirit became an inspiration of cour-
> age to the whole world.
>
> —Reverend W. C. Geisler, eulogist for Ida Lewis

The life of lighthouse keepers in general could be described as arduous, mundane, and, above all, lonely. Many of the light-houses of the nineteenth century were built in the middle of bodies of water on small islands that were constantly battered by elements such as gale-force winds. The houses and light-houses themselves were usually damp and drafty. The smell of mildew clung to the edifices, and something was always in need of repair. Maintenance extended to all the buildings. The storms, as well as sea or lake air, set to work on the paint and wood, making it peel or rot. It took a stalwart person to endure long periods of isolation.

Compared to other lighthouse-keeping families, the Lewis family had it easier. Lime Rock was located only 220 yards from the shore (a little more than twice the length of a football field). This distance was easily spanned by a walking bridge when the lighthouse was ultimately sold in the 1920s and converted to a yacht club. Unlike other children of keepers, the younger Lewises were able to continue their education on the mainland with other children, reducing the isolation that other keepers' families were forced to endure.

Keeping a lamp trimmed, bright, and effective was an involved and detail-laden task, much harder than it appeared. Shoals, rocks, and ledges were particularly hazardous to ships and boats. Failure to maintain the light properly could result in a perilous and deadly shipwreck, especially during a gale, storm, or hurricane. Mariners and seafaring vessels depended heavily on the lights cast by these navigational aids. It's hard to imagine their importance today, given the incredible advances in maritime science during recent decades. Then, however, mariners had to rely greatly on their own innate knowledge and experience. Primary navigation was done by the night sky.

Lighthouses of the mid-nineteenth century used lamps fueled by whale oil. Depending on the time of year, the viscosity of the oil changed: thinner during the summer because of the effects that heat had on the oil, and thicker during the winter months because of the frigid temperatures. If the oil was too thick, it had to be warmed to thin it out.

But maintaining the light was the most important aspect of any of the keeper's tasks. The quality of the light depended on how well the wick was trimmed and on how clean the panes of glass were. Therefore, Ida had to be sure to clean all the panes of the light, both inside and out. The wick was multi-hollow and the lamp was encased in a Fresnel lens of the sixth order, which designated that the size was the smallest made since they ranged from one to six. It stood 17 inches in height and

11¾ inches in diameter, which was more than suitable for the harbor. (Fresnel lenses were categorized by six orders, or sizes, the first being the largest at 7 feet 10 inches in height and 73⅙ inches in diameter, and sixth being the smallest, the size of the one that hung at Lime Rock.)

Fresnel lenses were invented in 1822, but it wasn't until 1840 that the first lenses were installed in U.S. lighthouses. Lime Rock, built in the 1850s, had a Fresnel lens. The circular, beveled-glass lenses and prisms on the top and the bottom refracted the light, which was intensified by a magnifying glass positioned in the middle of the lens. It cast the beam of light farther than the lanterns that had been developed until that point. The Fresnel lens was accompanied by a mechanical lamp, which burned oil that was pumped up from a reservoir below the level of the burner by means of weighted clockworks. The mechanism had to be taken care of, especially in the salt air, which tended to exact its toll on most metalwork.

In most lighthouse towers, the area at the top of the lighthouse that enclosed the lens, or "lanthorn" as it was known in Ida's time, was called the lantern room. Lime Rock's lantern room was part of the house, so Ida didn't have to leave home to tend to it. It was located on the second floor of the whitewashed stone home. The light was located in its own small room, complete with thick glass enclosure on all sides except the one facing the interior of the house.

Because of its skyrocketing cost, whale oil was replaced with lard in the late 1850s. Smaller lights used mineral oil, and alternative fuels—including wild cabbage, fish, olives, and finally kerosene in the 1870s—were experimented with. The keeper was instructed to wear a linen smock so that the more commonly worn wool would not scratch the optic (lens). Ida was required to clean the exterior of the lantern panes, clean the optic with spirits of wine (vinegar), and keep carbon and other grit from gathering on the glass. Once a year or so, the keeper needed to clean the lens with rouge, a nonscratching substance. The keeper also had to clean the chimney of the lamp, always making sure that spare clean lamps and chimneys were on hand (usually two). Finally, the keeper had to wind the clock weight and, if needed, clean and oil the clockworks.

All of these preparations for the coming evening had to be completed by 10:00 a.m. Then in the evening, the keeper would check the wind direction and adjust the vents to allow just enough draft into the lantern room. The entering draft would rise along the interior sides of the lantern panes, keeping them from fogging, to the top of the lantern. Wind passing horizontally through the ball vent would create a vacuum that pulled the draft up to the top of the lantern. This created a draft in the vent tube, which sucked the fumes from the oil-burning lamp, up the tube, to the ball, and out of the lantern room. The vent tube was made of metal and was directly attached to the glass chimney of the lamp.

The job didn't end when the light was lit at dusk. During the course of the evening, the keeper was required to wind the weights at least once, trim the wicks of the lamp as necessary, and adjust the vents so that a proper draft was present at all times. The chimney of the lamps had to be cleaned as well so that carbon buildup and soot didn't clog the chimney or create a backdraft.

And then there was the weather. Two decades before Lime Rock Lighthouse was completed, a fierce storm ripped through the harbor. A powerful bolt of lightning hit Lime Rock, destroying part of the island and further scattering the rocks. Ida often talked about the winds and torrential rains, which were amplified by the open, unprotected sea: "Sometimes the spray dashes against these windows so thick I can't see out, and for days at a time the waves are so high that no boat would dare come near the rock, not even if we were starving."

In addition to maintaining the light and keeping up the home, which had to be whitewashed almost every year, Ida had to keep track of the supplies needed to do her job. This included oil, cleaning supplies, additional lamps, and a vast array of brushes that aided the keeper in her morning tasks. There was a long list of instructions that accompanied the morning cleaning after the wick was extinguished. The brushes varied in length and purpose, such as feather brushes to carefully clean off the optics and a camel hair brush to polish rouge on the prisms and silver reflectors, if there were any. Silverplate brushes cleaned the lamps and utensils, removed excess rouge, and cleaned the revolving machinery, which was made of brass and copper. These brushes were also used to apply tar on ironwork, a particularly disgusting task. Bottle brushes with wire-stemmed handles were used to clean the glass chimneys of the lamps and the lamp burners.

Ida and her mother kept the brushes neatly on the shelving that lined the small cubicle-shaped lantern room, along with the other supplies needed to meticulously keep the lantern dust-free and aglow.

Many families had it much worse than the Lewises and lived in complete isolation, away from the conveniences of civilization, because of the treacherous elements of nature. Abbie Burgess was one of them. Abbie, a contemporary of Ida's who moved with her family to a lighthouse when she was fourteen, had a different life with which to contend. Maine, which was sparsely populated and intensely rustic, was hardly Newport. Compared to the harsh, brutal winters off the coast of Maine, life on the island of Lime Rock in Narragansett Bay was fairly easy. Abbie's charge was Matinicus Rock Light, located off the rough coast of Maine, about midway to the New Brunswick border.

The Lighthouse Board described the setting: "There is neither tree nor shrub, and hardly a blade of grass. The surface is rough and irregular and resembles a confused pile of loose stone. Portions of rock are frequently swept over by waves which move the huge boulders into new positions."

Matinicus Rock was stuck four miles off the south end of Matinicus Island, some twenty miles from the mainland. This lonely, desolate patch of tumbled rocks and boulders provided an excellent vantage point for ships and vessels rounding the continent and entering the treacherous shoals and ledges of the bay. The spot was home to two forty-eight-foot exposed lighthouse towers. From her youth until well into her thirties, Abbie kept not one lamp, but twenty-eight.

Abbie was fond of writing letters. When a winter storm blew in, the mighty Atlantic unleashed havoc on the dwelling and the surrounding animal pens. She described the scene: "Early in the day, as the tide rose, the sea made a complete breach over the rock, washing every movable thing away, and of the old dwelling not one stone was left upon another of the foundation."

The friend to whom she was writing must have once expressed a romantic wish to experience the angry ocean on the naked island, for Abbie wrote:

> *I was back in the house with the door fastened but none too quick for at that instant my little sister, standing at the window, exclaimed, "Oh, look! Look there! The worst sea is coming!" That wave destroyed the old dwelling and swept the Rock. I cannot think you would enjoy remaining here any great length of time for the sea is never still and when agitated, it roars, shuts out every sound, even drowning our voices.*

It was through the roar of the waves that Ida had developed a keen sense of perception, able to hear the cries of those going down in the water just outside her island. But it was more than that. For it took strength of character and the heart of a heroine to actually go to their rescue.

Chapter 6

THE RESCUES CONTINUE: THE SECOND, THIRD, AND FOURTH

Ever Just and Right, Angel of the Light House, Ida. In this world there's none beside her, none more true, more brave. In the tempest, on the wave, none more sure to save!

—AUTHOR UNKNOWN

Jones Bridge was a small projecting wharf that stuck out like a little finger into Newport Harbor, pointing directly at Lime Rock. At the end of the wharf, which was a good two hundred yards from the island, Ida's brother kept his skiff. It was particularly wet and cold in February 1866, with the remnants of winter lingering and the prospect of warmer spring weather not yet in sight. Newport's harbor settled down during the winter, but as it was the hub of commerce and general transportation, it still bustled with activity, inclement weather or not. Sitting out in the middle of Newport Harbor, Lime Rock endured not only the chilly precipitation but also the element of wind. After almost ten years on Lime Rock, Ida and her family had been forced to get used to the temperament of the sea and adjust to the winter chill that often clung to the inside of their stone house.

And it so happened this particular night that a group of three soldiers, drunk and reeling, were making their way from the local pubs back to Fort Adams. The fort was situated on the point of a small peninsula sticking into the harbor to the west of Lime Rock. The brownish-red garrison was easy to see from the lighthouse, as it was built up on the banks of the peninsula. It was a solid structure encompassing twenty-one acres. Seeing no action during the Civil War and it being winter, life at the fort was spent in mundane activities such as maintenance and repairs.

Drinking had become a problem among the soldiers stationed there. Years before, in 1836, the Grand Jury of Rhode Island District ruled that card playing and drunkenness within the fort were breaches of law. Although "ardent spirits" were prohibited on U.S. property, shanties had been set up just outside the fort for the sale of liquor, and the string of pubs in town and along the harbor fueled the soldiers as well.

Upon seeing a moored skiff and then eyeballing the long walk home (which was circuitous at best), the soldiers decided to borrow or steal the little boat and row their way across the large pocket of water to the garrison. It so happened that the boat belonged to Ida's brother. Rowing back to the fort was indeed a more direct route, provided that they were sober enough to handle the boat and that they could swim. (Swimming would not come into fashion as a widespread sport until the early twentieth century. Most people in the mid-1850s used water for bathing and splashing, rather than competitive swimming. It was considered more a show of athletics, rather than a need or a hobby. Many of those Ida rescued might have been able to swim the hundred or so yards to the lighthouse or shore, if they had been adept swimmers.)

When the three soldiers pushed off from the wharf heading toward the fort, they managed to get the boat into deep waters. No sooner had the jolly party reached the deepest part of the harbor than one of the soldiers, trying to stand up, shoved his foot through the bottom of the boat. It quickly filled with the icy water of the February sea. Two of the men must have leaped from the sinking vessel into the frigid water and struggled to swim toward shore. Perhaps they never made it to shore, or if they did, they went AWOL, for they never appeared back at the fort, nor did they turn up for bugle call. Their bodies were never found, and history chooses to log their destiny as having deserted the army.

The third drunken soldier was stuck with his foot wedged in the bottom of the boat. To make matters worse, the sinking boat was quickly being drawn out into the open sea by the tides. Oddly, it was within about fifty feet of Ida's first rescue of the four capsized boys eight years earlier. Looking out on the horizon, Ida's keen eyes saw her brother's drifting boat. She dashed outside to her small rowboat, which was tied to the Lime Rock dock, and seized the oars.

Within minutes she maneuvered the skiff to the wreck, working herself around to its stern. She reached overboard to hook the inebriated, semiconscious man by the arm onto the boat, hoping to drag him to the island. But she was forced to pull his unresponsive body slowly into the skiff. Using all of her strength and persistence, she tugged at the soaked, frozen man as he wailed drunkenly for help. She was able to topple him into the back end of the boat, loosening his foot from the sinking wreck.

During that rescue, Ida wrenched her back as the man's dead weight and stupor almost caused him to pull her into the depths with him. Exhausted and in pain, Ida managed to get into the back end of her skiff and rowed him back to her home at the lighthouse, where he was well fed and given a change of clothes. In reminiscing about the incident, she recalled that her physical injury took more than a year to heal and she never heard from the soldier again. To make matters worse, she said, "He never returned the clothing."

This was to be the scenario for most of Ida's rescues. She had to wait until her fifth rescue to receive any appreciation or acclaim. The young soldier was hardly grateful. At the time of the rescue, she was barely the same age at which acclaim was heaped upon Grace Darling, the woman with whom Ida would be forever linked.

As was Ida's custom, she never spoke of the heroic rescue. She would remain obscure and unknown, among the ranks of so many other female lighthouse keepers of her time, who went about their grueling lives in relative anonymity.

Less than a year later, on another cold wintry morning in January 1867, Ida's rescue skills were once again tested.

August Belmont was one of the elite of Newport. Belmont was a banker who owned an elaborate estate in town. He also owned sheep. And like many of his class, he had hired Irish farmhands to help maintain his fields.

Immigration to Newport was fueled by the shipbuilding industry. The Irish had come to work in the shipyards and were solicited to help build the fort and work on the farms. They eventually made up a significant portion of the population in what is now Newport's Fifth District.

A southeast gale was blowing that January morning at around 9:00 or 10:00. And three Irish farmhands were moving a valuable, prize-winning sheep for Belmont down Main Street, when it suddenly broke away from them and trotted toward the shore. The three followed and tried to corral the animal, but it plunged directly into the harbor, right off Jones Wharf. Desperate, the three watched their charge drifting slowly out toward Lime Rock.

On shore, the farmhands raced alongside the floating, bleating animal. Ida's brother had purchased a new skiff, which he kept tied up on the wharf, the former one being lost in the previous year's rescue of the drunken soldier. Spotting the boat, they leaped into it. Hardly seafaring men, the three tried desperately to paddle after the drifting sheep in the middle of the blustering winds, fighting the cresting waves that tossed the boat about.

Inexperienced sailors, the men knew they were in trouble. The waves came crashing over the edge of the boat, and the skiff began to take on water. The three men began to panic and started to shout for help. The vessel capsized, and all three fought to cling to its hull. Ida had been sewing in the kitchen near a window when she heard the frantic yells over the howling wind. She saw her brother's boat topple sideways and all three men go under a wave.

Ida wasted no time in getting into her rescue craft. She dipped the oars expertly into the choppy waves and dipped her chin into her chest as she moved through the water toward the screaming men, whose numb hands were losing their grip on the slippery hull. Ida recalled their cries, laced with Gaelic dialect. As she got closer, she could hear their Irish brogue as they prayed out loud to the deities and begged for their lives. "Oh Holy Virgin, and be Jabbers, have you come to save me?" one man called to her with a terrified look. The wind whipped around her and rain bit into her hands as she helped them into the skiff. Shivering and gushing appreciation, they begged to be dropped off back on shore, hoping to recapture their charge. Once she had landed them back on solid ground, they pleaded with her to rescue the runaway sheep. Fearful of their boss's wrath, they were near hysteria.

Ida relented. She shoved away from the shore and headed back into the crashing waves toward the struggling sheep, who was fighting weakly against the currents that were moving it toward open sea. Ida dug her oars in deeper and moved the skiff up beside the sinking animal. With great difficulty, she braced her feet against the slippery sides of the boat. With her hand lassoed around a length of rope, she bent into the waves to hook the loop around the beast's neck. The sheep, swallowing water and afraid, would not comply.

Ida regrouped several times, struggling to keep herself anchored in the rowboat, while keeping her back to the fierce wind and rain. Finally, she was able to secure the rope around the frenzied animal's neck, and with a wrench on the rope, she secured it to the side of the boat. Trying to pull the animal over the stern into the boat would have been too much, even for Ida Lewis. She rowed the boat, sheep in tow, into shore.

The farmhands wept with appreciation. But the appreciation ended there. Ida never heard from the farmhands again, nor did she hear from August Belmont. No one ever made any compensation to her for saving his prize sheep's life.

Her fourth rescue was not far behind. Just two weeks later, she was called to duty again. The underwater terrain between Lime Rock and the town had several rock masses, which would become exposed during the ebbing tides. One of these sunken rocks was marked with a spindle, or stick, which jutted out from the water. It was meant to warn sailors and pleasure craft of the rock's whereabouts.

But it was midnight. Maybe the boatman did not see the spindle in the darkness, even with the light from the nearby beam. Perhaps he just ignored it, being unfamiliar with the area and not realizing that its purpose was to ward him away from danger. As he was sailing into the harbor, his sailboat struck the rock head-on. Aided by the tide, which was starting to come into the harbor, the boat wedged itself on the jagged tip of the rock. A winter nor'easter was moving in and gaining strength. The cold water flowed around the sailor, who began to scream for help. His cries were drowned out by the wind and icy rain that rushed around him. His entreaties were lost in the expanse of water that ended where the crush of waves smacked against the shore of the small lighthouse island.

As the hours ticked by toward dawn, it was all the sailor could do to hang on. He struggled not to be washed away as he clung to the rigging, frozen saltwater stiffening his joints and locking them into position around the mast. The tide had crept in through the darkness of the night. The light from Lime Rock cast a safe glow in the distance as Ida and her family slept. With the rising water line and bitingly cold waves, he attempted to inch up higher, certain that death was upon him.

As dawn neared, the gray sky brightened, but the rains continued. Around 6:00 a.m., Ida's mother rose to check the lantern. She moved to the kitchen to light the fire in the hearth, and with a cursory glance out of the kitchen window, she saw the very top of the mast of the submerged boat. A closer look revealed the head of a man. The water had risen to just under his chin, and he was gulping for air as waves crashed over his head, forcing him to hold his breath. With a scream, she roused her daughter, who quickly put on her clothes and slipped into the rowboat at the base of the island.

He must have heard her call in the dawn air, as she yelled to him to hold on. She was on the way. Within minutes, her swift oar strokes brought her skiff to the sunken rock and the sailor, who was minutes away from becoming completely submerged under the tide. Ida hauled his frigid, water-logged body into the stern of the skiff. Hypothermia had set in, and when he hit the bottom of the boat, he was completely unconscious. Without panicking, Ida worked to revive him. He slowly came to, sputtering up sea water and working his arms spastically to bring back feeling. Satisfied that he was conscious, she angled her oars toward the warmth of her home. But he begged her to reverse direction and to take him to the wharf on shore. She tried to convince him otherwise and pressed him to allow her family to feed him breakfast and give him a change of clothing. But he was unrelenting, and she gave in to his request, assuming that he might not be right in the head. She deposited him on terra firma. She never heard from the man again. His name was never known.

Some weeks later, Ida received a note from the owner of the wrecked sailboat. Instead of a thank-you, the polite missive stated that he gladly would have given Ida $50 if she had let the man drown. Apparently he had stolen the boat.

Chapter 7

LOSING HEART

Not in the clamor of the crowded street
Not in the shouts and plaudits of the throng
But in ourselves, our triumph and defeat.

—Henry Wadsworth Longfellow

The years were beginning to weigh heavily on Ida. She had, in essence, been the lighthouse keeper of Lime Rock since her father's stroke. Even with her mother's assistance, she bore the brunt of the responsibility for her family. Her primary focus, however, was the light. The lantern had to be meticulously maintained as well as kept lit. Although her mother had toiled in the early years to keep the light, she now had other worries. Ida's sister Hattie, who was never healthy as a child, had grown into frail adulthood. Her lungs were weak and prone to infection, and Zoradia, herself crippled by chronic joint pain and easily fatigued, had to tend to her constantly and leave most of everything else on Ida's shoulders.

Ida found herself back at Lime Rock a little more than two years after her wedding. She was elated to return to the peace and contentment she found on her island home. But with her arrival came the sinking realization that she would take her place as titular head of the household. Although she had longed to be reunited with the lantern and the fine tasks of keeping it nightly, she realized that she faced nothing more than a life of manual servitude.

Her father had passed away in 1872, after years of being an invalid. At the end of his life, he had to have his food cut and fed to him. His passing came almost as a relief to the family. Zoradia took over as keeper after his death. As was the custom, she assumed the position in name so as to continue receiving a salary. But it was Ida who continued to keep the light. Her mother was no doubt wholly relieved to have capable, stalwart Ida back home. However, it was beginning to bother Ida that after years of being the keeper of the light, and being referred to as such in newspaper articles, she still was not appointed.

Her father had been crippled only four months after moving to Lime Rock in 1857. At that time, her mother was more helpful and did most of the tending to the light. Zoradia should have been appointed in her husband's stead. But it wasn't until his death in 1872 that her mother appears in the records as keeper, with no official appointment. Her mother wasn't the keeper; Ida was, and had been for a long time. Would Ida have to wait until the unfortunate death of her mother until finally receiving her rightful recognition?

The years were passing slowly, marked mainly by routine. With each passing summer came the onslaught of curiosity seekers. Even though Ida was used to them, she never welcomed them. She treated the visitors as part of her job and dutifully gave tours and answered questions. Gifts continued to pour in, and Ida appreciated all of them. The local newspapers seemed to keep a running tally, reporting on strange requests and gifts that were out of the ordinary. In 1870, months before her wedding, she received a pair of lace white stockings from the Chicago White Sox. The *Boston Journal* called the $500 gift, which had the emblem of the "great American game" embroidered on them in spun gold, a "perfectly useless gift." The paper continued:

Like the majority of her presents . . . a box of good English hose would have been more acceptable. Presents keep pouring in, flowers, dogs, silver, flags, etc., of no use to her. The salary of a harbor lighthouse keeper is not too much. . . . The silk flag framed on her wall is a nice thing to look at and the medals are very pretty to handle. The sewing machine she could not get time to use, and the beautiful boat has lain idle from want of strength to use the oars. Of cash she had very little and flowers and canary birds were not of much value.

Ida was fast becoming fodder for celebrity-style gossip in the papers, which led to some outlandish reports about her life. One report stated that contrary to popular belief, Ida could not swim. Another stated that she had left the lighthouse to work in a restaurant.

But regardless of whether she had the official appointment, she continued her vigilance over the waters and on numerous occasions set her skiff out on the billowy sea to aid mariners and others in trouble. Not all of Ida's rescues and selfless acts of bravery were recorded. Lack of eyewitnesses and Ida's own modesty kept them from getting the attention they deserved. She was never one to tout her own rescues, so they were always brought to the public's attention by someone else. It is difficult to know how many lives were actually saved, but even the briefs in the local papers point to a substantial number more than the documented eighteen.

During the 1870s, Ida's life developed into a routine centered on her beloved lantern. But growing slowly inside her was a deep resentment. The government never once considered officially appointing her lighthouse keeper. Her mother had assumed the job, as did so many other women, taking over the position handily but with no formal recognition from the government. The reason for this was mainly financial. There was no pension in place for appointed lighthouse keepers, who were always men. When they passed away or were disabled, their wives, daughters, or unmarried sisters would take over the position and continue to receive the annual salary. Unlike their husbands, these women's appointments never had to go through the official appointment process.

The first female lighthouse keeper that history remembers is Hannah Thomas, who lived with her husband at Plymouth Harbor in the late 1700s. When her husband was called to military duty to fight the British in the American Revolution, Hannah was left to tend the lights alone. Most lighthouses had gardens and animals to help offset food costs. Often, male lighthouse keepers ran other businesses off the island, such as fishing, oystering, or clamming. When they traveled to the nearest shore town to do business or sell their harvests, their wives had to tend the lights for weeks at a time.

Repairs had to be made, records kept, and supplies ordered. All of this fell on the wife or family, especially if the keeper was ill or aging. If the wife chose not to stay on, she would maintain the light until her husband's replacement arrived. By the mid-1800s it was becoming more and more common to have female keepers. By the early twentieth century, 211 women had been appointed lighthouse keepers, and twice that number were assistant keepers, frequently daughters or wives.

But this wasn't enough for Ida. She was not the keeper; her mother was. And when her mother died, the job most likely would be passed on to her. But it did not come as an official recommendation with the same meaning as if she had been a man, appointed in her own right.

This had become increasingly important to Ida, and for reasons lost to time, the whole matter began to wear on her. Perhaps her celebrity status, which was no longer at a fever pitch but did manage to keep her in the local papers, was actually a double-edged sword. Although she never asked for recognition, the fact that it landed on her doorstep made her think more seriously about her acts of bravery. It was not as if fame went to her head, but she continued to be celebrated as the most famous lighthouse keeper in the world, easily surpassing England's Grace Darling. She must have wondered why no recognition came to her from the government.

By all accounts, Ida was a modest and retiring person, often shrugging off her acts of unsurpassed bravery as if they were nothing. After all, lifesaving was considered part of the job. The Lighthouse Service rarely published details and barely mentioned rescues in its annual reports: "During the fiscal year, services in saving of life and property were rendered and acts of heroism performed by employees of the Lighthouse Service on vessels or at stations on ___ occasions," with the total being filled out for that given year.

There was something more, however. For beneath the stoic disregard of her feats, Ida had come to believe in the person whom the media and society had created. This is not to say that she was an arrogant person or suffered from an inflated ego. However, it was only human to get somewhat swept away in the face of the publicity and public adoration showered upon her in the course of less than five years. She felt she was more than deserving of the appointment that continued to elude her.

It might have been something even more basic. Although claiming no interest in or opinion about the women's rights movement, perhaps Ida was beginning to feel firsthand the sting of being passed over, ignored, or merely patted on the head for a job well done. In her own mind, she had to know that the courage she demonstrated during her numerous rescues was uncommon, even for a man. Though she may have drawn no distinction in her mind of the difference between men and women when it came to life's tasks, perhaps it began to dawn on her that the rest of the world did. Being treated as the eldest son by her father may have instilled in her this sense of equality. It was expected that she do all the tasks that a boy, and then a man, would. When did the roles change?

"Anyone who thinks it is un-feminine to save lives has the brains of a donkey," Ida said. She had been compared to a man in many instances and by many writers. An article in *Ladies' Home Journal* entitled "Ida Lewis at Home," which ran in its July 1890 issue, was one of many that drew this analogy:

> *It is almost everyone's first surprised comment, spoken or not, expecting to see a female Hercules. Her eyes are a clear, honest blue gray, her face rather severe in repose, brightens in speech, and shows where a few unusual dimples lurk. Her firm, square jaw is an index of the strength of will that has made it possible for her to brave peril that many a strong man would decline. Fate does not often throw in one person's path, to be sure, so many opportunities to distinguish oneself for heroism, but it is not everyone who would have accepted them all so promptly.*

And accept it she did, time and again.

In November 1877 Ida's bravery was once against tested on the waters of Newport Harbor. This particular incident involved three soldiers who were musicians in the band at Fort Adams. Winter and alcohol seemed to bring out the worst in them, and once again, a groggy trio decided to take a boat home, rather than travel by foot. No sooner had they gotten the skiff into deep water than it capsized.

Not much is known of this rescue, except that Ida was quick to jump in her boat and drop her oars in the white peaks of the sea. She did this with such ferocity that she made it to the wreck in record speed. However, hauling the soggy men, combined with the falling winter snow, proved to be exhausting. The boat's load was so heavy that she had to stop several times on the perilous journey back to the house to recover her strength.

The rescue proved to be too much for Ida. She became sick with what is suspected to be diphtheria, a bacterial throat infection that causes a thick membranous substance to form, making it difficult to breathe and swallow. The strain of the rescue, compounded with exposure to the icy seas and winds, left her with a high fever and general weakness. Month after month, Ida lay still, using her energy only to clean the lantern and perform some light housework.

Newspaper articles began to ponder her future. Ida still had not been officially appointed lighthouse keeper, and she was making no money of her own. For the first time, there was talk of a pension, something to help her subsist in her old age, when she was no longer able to rescue drunken soldiers, way-ward lads, or runaway sheep. The fact that the government, despite all the attention this modern-day heroine had garnered, did nothing to officially recognize her was demoralizing.

The government's failure to appoint Ida assumed insulting proportions.

෨෬

By mid-1878 Ida finally recovered from her long sickness. On April 18 of that year, the family rowed to the mainland to celebrate brother Hosea's (Hosey's) marriage to twenty-three-year-old Ellen Moran. She was an Irish Catholic girl who had been born in England. As was the custom of the time, the religion of the wife was respected, so the wedding was celebrated at St. Mary's Catholic Church. Hosea was twenty-eight and a teamster, having turned his back on pursuing a life on the water like his father and sister. He was plagued with ill health and weak lungs like his sister Hattie, so living on the water was not the best place for him. Hosea and his bride moved to a small house in downtown Newport.

The next year, Ida felt the diphtheria coming on again. The local newspaper, the *Newport Mercury*, reported that she "remembered that kerosene was an unfailing remedy" and lauded her quick thinking. Having gallons of it on hand to fuel the lantern, she swallowed an entire tablespoon, which of course forced her to vomit violently. Then she saturated a cloth in the noxious fuel and wrapped it around her throat. She continued to do this several more times, until she felt she had killed the diphtheria and fell into an exhausted sleep.

She had warded off the illness.

Throughout the 1870s, Ida became known to and acquainted with some very powerful people, and those influential men would eventually serve her well.

Ida had never actually met General Ambrose Everett Burnside, the Civil War general known for making sideburns popular. Burnside served as governor of Rhode Island after the war and in 1874 was elected to the U.S. Senate. Word of Ida's November 1877 rescue reached his ear, as did her lack of appointment to the position of lighthouse keeper. Sometime in 1878 he decided to champion her cause and inquired among the authorities why Ida Lewis, famed heroine of Lime Rock, was still not appointed as lighthouse keeper. No one could answer his question.

Outraged at the slight to this brave woman who had been faithfully discharging her duties without pay or title, Burnside started making noise.

As the *New York Times* would later report in a retrospective on her life that ran October 29, 1911, entitled "The Passing of Ida Lewis, the Heroine of Newport":

> *She would not have got the position had it not been for the rescue of three intoxicated musicians who were just disappearing under the waves. . . . The famous general's sense of justice was revolted and he didn't rest until he had obtained the title as well as the duties of the office. It was almost the last act of his life.*

On January 21, 1879, Ida finally received the appointment for which she had been waiting so long. It had been arranged by Burnside and ushered along by her political connections in the U.S. Navy and Lighthouse Bureau. Signed by Secretary of the Treasury John Sherman, the official letter read:

> *You are hereby appointed Keeper of the Lighthouse at Lime Rock, R.I., at a salary of $750 per annum, vice Mrs. Zoradia Lewis resigned. This appointment is conferred upon you as a mark of my appreciation for your noble and heroic efforts in saving human lives.*

Ida had almost given up all hope. She must have heard in 1878 that the appointment was going through, for she sent a note to Burnside with the pending news in the early summer, to which he responded on July 1, 1878. In his own handwriting on a small U.S. Senate postcard, rimmed with the black border of mourning (indicating the recent death of his wife), he wrote:

> *My dear Mrs. Wilson*
>
> *I thank you for your kind letter of the 30th last. It gave me great pleasure to be of service to you, particularly as you so well deserve all that the government has done for you. I wish it could do more. With wishes for your health and happiness, I remain very truly yours, AE Burnside.*
>
> *If you will kindly send the letter from the Lighthouse Board to me, I will take copy of it and return the original to you.*

The appointment came just before what many consider to be the most perilous rescue of Ida's life and one that would garner her a second wave of worldwide recognition and renewed fame. Ida was finally and officially the keeper of Lime Rock.

൙

Deep winter was always an unpleasant time on Lime Rock. Gale-force winds off the Atlantic Ocean were often accompanied by roiling black waves and the raw, bone-biting temperatures that only wet winter can bring. To make matters worse, in late winter during that era, massive chunks of ice often drifted into the harbor, isolating the small lighthouse island in its own frozen tundra. The repeating cycle of daytime sun

An artist's rendition of Newport Harbor in the late 1800s. Note Lime Rock Lighthouse on the right. *Courtesy of Ida Lewis Yacht Club*

This popular portrait shows Ida with a scarf worn fichu style. *Harper's Weekly* replicated this pose in a cover illustration.
Courtesy of Ida Lewis Yacht Club

An illustration from *Frank Leslie's Illustrated Newspaper* featuring Ida in the *Rescue* after the dedication ceremony on July 4, 1869.
Courtesy of Ida Lewis Yacht Club

Ida Lewis's birthplace in Newport. The Lewis family lived here and Hosea commuted twice daily to the light, until the house was built on Lime Rock.
Bernard J. Skomal, from the Author's Collection

Ida Lewis posed often in a lifeboat. Here she is photographed in her reliable skiff.
Courtesy of Ida Lewis Yacht Club

A postcard of Lime Rock Lighthouse circa late 1800s.
Courtesy of Ida Lewis Yacht Club

A portrait of Ida in her early fifties. The gold pin at her neck was a gift from the Sorosis Society. *Courtesy of Ida Lewis Yacht Club*

A replica of the Lime Rock lantern in the room where the light was located.
Bernard J. Skomal, from the Author's Collection

An illustration from *Harper's Weekly* showing Ida (center) with her mother and disabled father. *Courtesy of Ida Lewis Yacht Club*

Ida with her brother Rudolph on the deck of the lighthouse.
Courtesy of Ida Lewis Yacht Club

…da with Lime Rock Lighthouse in the background, late 1800s.
Courtesy of Ida Lewis Yacht Club

A rare photo of Ida smiling.
Courtesy of Ida Lewis Yacht Club

Trophy for the Ida Lewis Regatta.
Bernard J. Skomal, from the Author's Collection

The gravestone of Ida Z. Lewis,
located in the cemetery off
Farewell Street in Newport,
Rhode Island.
*Bernard J. Skomal, from the Author's
Collection*

and overnight freezing fused the small ice patches into a larger ice mass that often extended from the mainland out into the harbor. This phenomenon was so common that by February, locals knew where the safe spots ended and the thinner, more treacherous ice began.

Soldiers made up a significant portion of Newport's population. Those stationed at Fort Adams, like the rest of the town's residents, knew about the patches of ice that melded together to create seemingly safe walkways. They also knew the risk involved in walking beyond the few hundred feet of "safe ice" that paralleled the shore. Beyond that point the ice became somewhat thin and mushy, with spotty holes where the drift ice had not fully closed in.

However, knowledge of that danger didn't always lead to cautious behavior. At 5:00 p.m. on February 4, 1881, Giuseppe Gianetti and Freddie Tucker, both privates stationed at Fort Adams, set out on foot from town, where they had apparently been patronizing several grog houses, and headed toward the fort. Hoping to cut some time off their journey, they ventured onto the ice in the harbor, making their way past Lime Rock. They were so drunk that either they misjudged where the safe ice ended and patchy ice began or they just didn't care.

Ida and her family were preparing dinner in the kitchen of their small home on Lime Rock. Whether it was dinnertime or not, the kitchen was the preferred place to be, as the bitter chill easily penetrated the stone structure of the lighthouse. The small fireplace in the kitchen provided the most warmth in the home.

As the soldiers tromped over the crunchy ice into Bretton Cove, where the ice was notoriously thin, Ida and her mother caught sight of them from the window. At that moment, a loud, terrifying cracking noise cut through the air as the ice gave way under their weight. They slid into the murky, freezing depths below, disappearing from view. Their eerie screams pierced the twilight.

Ida's mother fainted, while Hattie rushed to tend to her. Without putting on either a coat or outer gear, Ida raced to the door and grabbed a clothesline. Hattie yelled for help to her brother Rudolph, who was in another part of the house. He followed after Ida a few minutes later.

Out on the ice, Ida raced toward the men, who were crying out in pain as the freezing Atlantic Ocean numbed their limbs. Wary of the condition of the precarious makeshift floor beneath her feet, she moved toward the floundering men gingerly, trying the ice with her shoe points. Once within striking distance, she tossed the clothesline to two sets of grasping hands.

It missed.

She reeled in the slack and tried again. She yelled that only one of them should grab hold at a time, but they obviously misunderstood her. Both soldiers grabbed the line. Ida drew in the slack and began to tug and pull the rope backward, using her slight weight and strong determination against their two bodies. She again yelled for one of them to let go. They began to panic, and Ida cinched the rope tighter. She moved even closer to the treacherous thin ice. She began to pull backward with all the strength in her arms and upper back, begging one of the men to release the cord.

They instead yanked forward on the clothesline. With a startling jerk, Ida plunged forward and stumbled onto the mushy ice, which easily gave way under her weight. Her skirts quickly filled like a balloon as her body was pulled into the harbor's icy depths. Her bustle, typical of the Victorian fashion of the time, further weighted Ida down. The air rushed out of her lungs as the shock of the frigid water hit her, and the steel fittings of her corset sent stabbing pains through her chest. She felt herself being pulled under by the weight of the struggling, sinking soldiers.

Quite characteristically, Ida managed to keep her wits about her. She slackened the clothesline. Luckily, she was a capable swimmer; in fact, she had been touted the best swimmer in Newport at the age of fourteen. Her skill served her well. Forcing her numb limbs into action, she moved her soaking body back to the edge of broken-away ice, never losing grip on the icy clothesline, and hauled herself up, edging forward until the ice could hold her weight.

Her sickly sister Hattie watched in horror from the kitchen window, while ineffectively nursing their mother back to consciousness. Ida was soaked to the skin, with more than ten yards of wet skirts clinging to her in below-freezing temperatures, as she tried to brace her slim body against the dead weight of the drunken soldiers. Finally, one of the soldiers relinquished his hold on the rope, allowing Ida to save the other man.

Propelled to action, she lost no time once afoot. She caught up the slack on the clothesline and, with concentrated might, pulled the sinking man toward her. With one final heave, she slid his torso onto the stronger ice and then managed to drag him onto solid footing.

At this point, her brother Rudolph arrived, and together they used the clothesline and their combined strength to pull the second soldier, now almost unconscious, out of the harbor. They brought the men back to the house to change clothes and warm themselves. Then they were transported to Newport Hospital for several days before being discharged.

Soon after that, newspapers latched onto Ida's latest act of bravery. Throughout the country, published accounts told how this slight woman, braced with unshakable courage, risked her own life to rescue the two soldiers. Recountings of the incident did not mention her brother.

A letter arrived shortly after the lifesaving, dated February 11, 1881. In thin, precise script on a small sheet of lined paper, a heartfelt note was penned by one of the soldiers' mothers:

Dear good brave woman. What can I say. What can I do for I cannot thank you half enough on paper for saving the life of my Dear Boy, Freddie O. Tucker. Only last Sunday, I was reading of your bravery in rescuing two men. I little thought one of them was my dear boy. I have always felt an [sic] desire to see you and if nothing happens then I will visit Newport this summer then I will see you. But if you are sick, you send for me. I will come and do for you. This is one of my wishes, I wish I was rich.

The second page of the letter is now lost. It is not known if Ida actually received the woman at the lighthouse or if she even responded to the letter. But it is one of the only surviving letters of gratitude that Ida ever received.

Ida spoke about the incident: "I was pretty strong then. It was hard work pulling those men out to strong ice, and it made my arms lame." About the source of her uncommon strength in the throes of that event, she said, "I don't know. I ain't particularly strong. The Lord Almighty gives it to me when I need it. That's all."

Despite her humility, this single act of bravery would not go unnoticed. U.S. Customs Collector John H. Cozzens, on hearing about the dangerous rescue, contacted the Lighthouse Board.

Ida first caught wind that something amazing was going to happen to her when she received correspondence from Rear Admiral John Rodgers on February 11, 1881, just days after the rescue. In it he told Ida that in 1874 Congress had passed legislation providing a medal for "recognition of such services to humanity and prescribing the evidence upon which it should be awarded." She was being nominated for the recognition. In the process, the lighthouse inspector would have to obtain and forward affidavits about the rescue, which would then be reviewed by the secretary of the Treasury.

Eyewitness accounts of that day were taken from everyone involved, including her mother, Hattie, the two soldiers saved, and the commanding officer at the fort. They all concurred that Ida's rescue put her in great peril and at risk of serious injury. As a result, Ida was honored with a gold Life Saving Medal of the First Class for her heroism.

The following September, the medal was transmitted to her, and with it came a formal letter from Secretary of the Treasury William Windom, who wrote:

These deeds have already won for you national distinction, and it is peculiarly appropriate that you should receive the national lifesaving medal in commemoration of your brave acts as a life saver, while it is an occasion for added satisfaction that such a memorial of unquestionable heroism should have been won by a woman.

At noon on October 11, 1881, the official presentation was made, with both Collector Cozzens and former Collector Seth Macy present, as well as the mayor and other city dignitaries. Ida Lewis was accompanied by her sister Hattie. As Ida sat and listened to the presentation, her hands were neatly folded in front of her, and on her dress she wore her Sorosis Society gold pin, neatly clipped at her throat. Doing the honor was French E. Chadwick, who was then a lieutenant with the U.S. Navy and who would turn out to be, along with his wife, a guardian angel for Ida. Chadwick said:

It is my pleasant duty to be the bearer to Mrs. Lewis of the highest token of merit of its kind which can be given in this country, the Life Saving Medal of the first class to be conferred by the United States Government for in the words of the law itself, extreme heroic daring, involving imminent personal danger on the part of the rescuer. . . . I would preface this by here recording the great modesty which Mrs. Lewis

*has shown in relation to her noteworthy acts: she has kept no
personal records of what she has done: has preserved none of
the many laudatory newspaper notices which have frequently
appeared regarding her, knew scarcely any of the dates of her
actions, and in most instances did not know the names even
of the men she had saved. This very unusual disregard of the
causes of her distinction was brought to light in the investi-
gations necessary to make an authentic report of her many
rescues to the Lighthouse Board.*

With that, he launched into an accounting of the rescues,
as best could be remembered and accounted for.

In the 1881 annual report of U.S. Life Saving Service,
Ida Lewis's write-up was extensive and culminated in praise
of her courage: "The action on her part showed unquestionable nerve, presence of mind, and dashing courage. . . . All
witnesses unite in saying the rescue was accomplished at the
imminent risk of the rescuer's life."

Since 1874, when Congress passed the act awarding
these medals to civilians, this was the first time that a woman
received the honor, which is reserved for exceptional bravery in rescuing lives. She also received a gold medal from the
Humane Society of the Commonwealth of Massachusetts,
which had never previously awarded honors to anyone outside of the state. Ida was the exception.

This was her second-to-last documented rescue, the documentation coming from a report compiled by the inspector himself in the process of obtaining the affidavits. It was
mainly Zoradia and Ida who, relying on memory, provided

evidence as to how many rescues Ida had actually performed to date. Recalling as many as she could and relying in part on Brewerton's account, Ida came up with what would be considered the official total at the end of her life: eighteen.

By this time, Ida was thirty-nine years old and had been the official lighthouse keeper for two years. She was also presented with a purse of gold coins and a silver teapot (which cost $150 at the time) in honor of the rescue. These gifts came from the soldiers and officers at Fort Adams. She often showed it off to visitors and displayed it prominently in her home. With the exception of the teapot and the silk flag presented to her by Jim Fisk on Independence Day 1869, Ida never displayed gifts. Rather, she kept them meticulously in a keepsake basket. They remained in the original containers in which she received them, the hinges on the cases rusting in the sea air. While they must have held some significance for her, she never took advantage of the entitlement that each one gave to her. That entitlement, along with the medals, also remained neatly tucked away.

Chapter 8

A SOLITARY LIFE (1881–1911)

I love it. I could not be contented elsewhere.

—IDA LEWIS, REFERRING TO LIFE ON LIME ROCK

Newport had long attracted the wealthy to its scenic shores, earning its reputation as a playground for the rich and famous. Drawn to Newport in the late 1800s, some of the country's wealthiest people inhabited the opulent mansions that dot the island's north shore. This was the era of the Industrial Revolution.

The country was between two great wars: the Civil War and World War I. It was literally a coming of age for the United States, for in a period of less than fifty years, the country transformed itself from a rural republic into an urban state. The frontier had vanished, and in its place, great factories and steel mills, transcontinental railroad lines, flourishing cities, and vast agricultural holdings marked the land. And with them came monopolies, brutal factory working conditions, slums, and a growing disparity between the very wealthy and the very poor.

The twenty or thirty years preceding the Civil War had laid the groundwork for the end of the century. The war had stimulated manufacturing and speeded up an economic process whose fundamental factors were the exploitation of iron, steam, and electrical power as well as the forward march of science and invention. The 36,000 patents granted before 1860 were but a drop in the bucket compared to the flood of inventions to follow. From 1860 to 1890, 440,000 patents were issued, and in the first quarter of the twentieth century, the number reached nearly a million.

During the nineteenth century, for example, Thomas Edison made practical use of electricity (1880); Samuel F. B. Morse perfected electrical telegraphy (1844), linking distant parts of the continent with a network of poles and wires; and Alexander Graham Bell exhibited a telephone instrument (1876). In addition, the tempo of business was quickened by the invention of the typewriter in 1867, the adding machine in 1888, and the cash register in 1897. The linotype composing machine, the rotary press, and paper-folding machinery made it possible to print 240,000 eight-page newspapers in an hour. The boon of invention and growth of big business and monopolies resulted in a new level of productivity in virtually all fields. And many of the major players chose very handsome trappings for themselves.

Elsie French Vanderbilt was one of them. A vibrant, schooled woman, she had what many considered the great fortune to marry Alfred Gwynne Vanderbilt, great-grandson of "Commodore" Cornelius Vanderbilt and son of Alice and Cornelius Vanderbilt. Born Ellen French Tuck in 1881, Elsie, as she was known, was the daughter of the president of the Manhattan Trust Company. The marriage occurred in the same year that Ida received the great honor of being singled out as the first woman to be awarded the gold U.S. Life Saving Medal.

The society papers described Elsie as "tall and divinely fair with a wealth of titian-coloured hair and brilliant complexion, made more beautiful by surf and sun." She spent much of her childhood growing up at Harbourview, an exquisite estate built by her parents on the shore of Newport, looking out at Lime Rock Light. Unlike the Vanderbilt family that she was to marry into, Elsie lived most of the time in Newport, rather than just the summers. Ida Lewis was already a legend during her childhood, and Elsie would look across the still waters of the harbor and wonder about the woman whom she could see only as a small spot on the island.

Newport's proximity to New York City, access to the ocean, bustling port, and attractive sweeps of landscape were a natural lure to the wealthy. The massive fortunes garnered during this period helped usher in the Gilded Age, which was punctuated by blatant political corruption in the 1870s. The period took its name from an 1873 novel by Mark Twain (in collaboration with Charles Dudley Warner), an essayist, humorist, and editor for *Harper's Magazine*. Considered to be a jab at the excesses of the time, the novel provided strong commentary on the era's political and social climate.

Summer homes had always been common among the well-to-do, as were traveling abroad and fine-tuning the social graces. However, their preoccupation with building monstrous homes in the grand style of European castles had just begun to manifest itself in the late 1800s.

Beechwood mansion had been built in 1851 by a New York City merchant named Daniel Parrish. John Jacob Astor, the German immigrant who made himself the richest man in

America by investing in fur trading and real estate, bought it in 1881 and poured $2 million into its renovation. It later became the home of William Backhouse Astor Jr., grandson of John Jacob Astor. William was married to the legendary Caroline Schermerhorn, who insisted on being called *The* Mrs. Astor, the undisputed queen of American society. A social snob of the utmost degree, she devised the famous Four Hundred, a list of 213 families and individuals whose lineage could be traced back at least three generations. The list is better known as the Social Registry, or Blue Book. Her son, John Jacob Astor IV, would go down in history as the wealthiest man to die on the *Titanic*.

For the eight weeks of summer that Mrs. Astor actually resided in the multimillion-dollar Beechwood mansion, she presided over the elite social activities that only the privileged could enjoy. The highlight of the summer was Mrs. Astor's Summer Ball; being invited to the event was the ultimate proof of one's social worth. It was the Astors who brought New York high society to Newport.

Keeping up with the Astors was no easy task, but the Vanderbilts had the power and the means to do so. In the late 1800s Cornelius Vanderbilt II, grandson of steamship and railroad tycoon "Commodore" Vanderbilt and chairman of the New York Central Railroad, purchased a large wood-frame summer cottage perched on a cliff overlooking the ocean. Following a fire, Cornelius tore down the home and replaced it in 1893 with what is the grandest of all the Newport mansions, The Breakers. The seventy-room Renaissance-style palazzo was inspired by sixteenth-century palaces of Genoa and Turin and was built predominantly of imported marble.

Perhaps Cornelius was influenced by his younger brother William and William's wife, Alva, who also decided to vacation in Newport in 1888. They chose to build a mansion from scratch rather than purchase one of the existing wood-frame, oversized cottages. They commissioned a fantastic mansion, made completely of marble, to replicate the Petit Trianon at Versailles. Marble House was finished in 1893 and marked the transformation of Newport from a quiet summer colony of wood-frame houses to a legendary resort community of stone homes. Though it was quaintly called a cottage, the $11 million (by contemporary cost accounts) mansion was the first of the Gilded Age homes to be completed. The 500,000 square feet of marble was said to cost $7 million of the total cost.

The Vanderbilts, the Astors, and a host of other captains of industry such as Edward Julius Berwind—a millionaire coal merchant and owner of another mansion, The Elms— put Newport on the social register. The twentieth century was just beginning.

This was the world in which Elsie French Vanderbilt was raised. It was the only Newport she knew, and the one she loved. Given that, she was still drawn to the other Newport— the one where Ida Lewis lived and worked.

It seemed just a matter of course that Elsie, given her attraction to Lime Rock and her fascination with this home-grown heroine, would venture out to the island to meet Ida. After their initial meeting, she was often rowed out to the island and spent time talking and visiting, while Ida continued her chores.

Even with their obvious age difference of almost forty years—Elsie was a teenager visiting the now-middle-aged heroine—Ida appreciated the company. Summertime was often chock-full of curiosity seekers and visitors, though the stream had abated somewhat over time. Ida looked forward to her young visitor who, with all the graciousness of well-heeled society, still spoke to her with the eagerness and interest of youth. They became friends.

Elsie was twenty years old when she married Vanderbilt in 1901. Their wedding was an opulent affair in typical Vanderbilt style. The ornate wedding cake was in the shape of a trolley, and within every slice was a keepsake piece of jewelry for each guest. The couple soon had a son, and Elsie spent more and more time away from her beloved island raising William Henry III. But when she did come back to visit, she made a point to spend time with her unlikely friend.

Ida had encountered the rich and famous, the legendary and the popular, countless times before. However, this was the first time in all of her years of being a public figure that she enjoyed the consistency of an actual friendship with someone whose life was so very different from her own. Elsie would prove to be a good friend, even after her divorce from Alfred in 1908. She and her son moved to Tuxedo, New York, while Alfred made the Plaza Hotel his new home. (Four years after Ida's death, Alfred would make a trip abroad on the ill-fated ship *Lusitania* and was one of the 1,201 people to drown in the sinking of that ship by a German submarine torpedo. Elsie eventually remarried and lived a full, active life in politics until her death in 1948 at the age of sixty-seven.)

While the Gilded Age in Newport flourished, Ida lived quite a different life, oblivious of the changes. Like many lighthouse keepers, she spent much of her time tending to her duties and maintaining the small home. She planted flowerbeds and kept pets, her favorites being cocker spaniels and cats. She was also burdened with nursing her ailing mother, who suffered from stiff joints and chronic pain, and Hattie, whose lung problems had developed into tuberculosis. Hosey, her youngest brother, had also developed tuberculosis and was being nursed on the mainland by his wife of five years. Her brother Rudolph was unmarried and still lived on Lime Rock, helping out as assistant keeper and spending some time at sea as a part-time captain.

Ida still made the papers periodically, especially when she participated in a rescue or assisted another mariner. Several accounts in the *Newport Daily News* detailed rescue attempts in which she participated but was aided by quicker, faster boats. And Newport Harbor was changing. More pleasure craft and yachts filled a bay that once used to moor only fishing vessels and rowboats. Yachting was becoming the sport of the wealthy, and the Gilded Age was in full swing. More and more people knew how to handle boats, and Ida was now one of many who could capably swing oars.

And she was getting older. Ida was forty-one when Hosey died on June 12, 1883. The death was expected, but untimely; it was followed later that year by the loss of Hattie, who also died of tuberculosis (which the medical books of the time referred to as consumption). The disease had taken its toll on both siblings, leaving them gaunt and deathlike in appearance. The deaths, especially Hattie's, deeply affected Ida, who dearly missed her sister. She once commented that she often felt her dead sister with her when she was out on her boat, Hattie's presence making the rowing much easier for her.

Her mother took to her bed following Hattie's death. She had developed cancer and remained an invalid for the remainder of her life. As it was, she had not left the island during the five years that Hattie was critically sick, tending the light only as much as her own illness would permit.

Hattie was the beauty of the family. She never married, most likely because of her illness. A friend wrote to the local newspaper the day after her death, recapping the closeness of Ida's relationship with her:

The two sisters were closely united in their affections and tastes. Hattie possessed rare beauty before her sickness, and was characterized by great amiability and equanimity. Retiring in disposition, the graces of her character were exhaled like the aroma of flowers on sea-girt rocks. Though long possessed of a reverent frame of mind, during her last sickness she obtained great peace in the profession of her faith in Christ, and her final dissolution was marked with peace and dignity.

Ida's own religious devotion coupled with Hattie's passing may have led Ida to her next decision.

In the following year Ida turned solidly toward religion. On June 8, 1884, she rowed to shore, walked into the Thames Street Methodist Episcopal Church, and was baptized. Although she had been a member of the temperance movement since her twenties and a follower of Christian dogma, the forty-two-year-old Ida had an underlying desire to make all things concerning her life official. She began to attend church daily, often spending the entire Sunday on shore if her brother Rudolph was home to tend the light. At night she and her mother would read the Bible together.

Before Zoradia's death, an article in the *New York Sunday Times* in the late 1880s spoke of the quiet life that Ida had settled into with her mother. The two rarely had visitors except in the summer, "but they are happy—happy in each other's love and daily read the well-worn family Bible and talk of those who have preceded them in the spirit land and with whom they expect to commune in the future."

When Zoradia died of cancer on July 16, 1887, it was a quiet death. She never awoke from her sleep, and Ida found her seventy-two-year-old mother in bed. She closed the door and quietly rowed to shore. Another chapter of her life had closed.

Without her mother and constant companion, Ida was now predominately alone.

∽

Although Rudolph was with her during the latter part of her life, Ida never relinquished full control of the light.

Her bedroom was located directly across from the tiny room that housed the lantern, which hung in the room and overlooked the ocean. Even in her sleep, she could sense when the wick needed trimming or when the light had dimmed, and she would make her way across the hallway and take the large step into the cramped four-by-four-foot quarters that housed the heavy lamp. Shelves lined the sides of the room and were stocked with brushes, cutting utensils, polishes, and oil. She would deftly clean the lantern glass and check the oil supply, making adjustments and lighting the beacon for the evening.

Ida said, "There's a peace on this rock that you don't find on shore. There are hundreds of boats going in and out of this harbor. It's part of my happiness to know they are depending on me to guide them safely."

By the last two decades of her life, Ida had won herself a comfortable place in history. She was considered by the press to be the "pet" of the government. In one brief, it was reported that she was receiving special treatment by not having to conform to the new Lighthouse Service rules, which mandated that all employees wear the new lighthouse keepers' uniforms. Although supposedly everyone had to wear the regulation uniform, the truth of the matter was that no woman in the employ of the Lighthouse Service was expected to wear the double-breasted, blue wool coat with yellow buttons, dark blue trousers, and cap bearing a metal lighthouse badge.

Although the newspapers may have inflated her status, it wasn't lost on those on the Lighthouse Board that she had admirers and protectors who adored her. She was already being paid more than any of her colleagues in the area. Records show that Gustave Clark, keeper of Rose Island Light, was making $500 a year; Charles Schoenemann at Newport Harbor Light, $600; and Frank Parmell at Castle Hill Light, $560.

Ida was being paid $750.

The relationships between keepers were generally friendly, however, and it is doubtful that her peers begrudged the aging Ida her salary, especially given her celebrity status and hard-earned reputation.

By 1896 President Grover Cleveland made some changes benefiting lighthouse keepers. He classified them as civil servants, which gave them protections they never had, including the chance for pensions and job stability. The practice of being kicked out of a lighthouse and being replaced by a new favored appointee was over, giving keepers a well-deserved sense of permanence.

Ida herself told of other rescues during the late nineteenth century and early twentieth century. She spoke of having saved two men and two children, who cried out for her by name as they clung to an overturned boat. "Ida, Ida Lewis, come save us," they called, which she readily did. She often enlisted the help of Rud on her adventures. Together she and her brother once spied a capsized vessel, which happened to belong to a local man, also named Lewis. They fished him out of the marshy area of the harbor, where he was knee-deep in mud and utterly exhausted. After he revived himself in their kitchen, he told them that after sailing all around the globe, he thought he was going to end up drowning in an old bog within sight of his home.

Ida had many such stories about the rescues that never made it past her lips. But Ida's efforts hardly went unnoticed, especially in the later years of her life. In 1906 two female friends were rowing out to see Ida. As she waited patiently for their arrival, one of the women stood to adjust her skirts and toppled into the water. She wasn't able to swim, and her companion couldn't pull her in. A sixty-four-year-old Ida dropped her lifeboat from its hanger and rowed across the water to complete her final documented rescue. (She is unofficially attributed with at least one more rescue three years later, when a group of five girls capsized their skiff and called for help. She was sixty-seven.)

Although 1906 proved to be a banner year for Ida, it would be one of the last before her star began to fall. Whether she realized it or not, she had a bevy of support and could count some powerful people as friends. One of them was Admiral George Dewey. Dewey, a hero of the Spanish-American War, had been appointed admiral in 1899, following an illustrious career in the navy. Ida had originally met him when he was first appointed president of the Lighthouse Board in the 1880s. He often came to visit her and was fond of their casual conversations. Being from Vermont, he took a strong liking to the Yankee character of this small, courageous woman. She named her cocker spaniel Dewey, in honor of their bond. Ida was also friends with Mrs. French E. Chadwick, who was the wife of Rear Admiral Chadwick, the man who had helped secure her appointment and bestowed the gold medal upon her.

Chadwick was well connected. His wife fretted that Ida's lack of a husband left her with no one to care for her when the inevitable time came that she would have to retire. A pension would help her immensely. At the time, philanthropist Andrew Carnegie had founded the Carnegie Hero Trust Fund, which recognized the efforts of those who put themselves in perilous situations to save others. In some cases, the fund gave compensation to those who risked their lives for others and also awarded a medal in honor of their deeds. Mrs. Chadwick wrote to Carnegie, who thought long and hard about Ida. Unfortunately, he could not add her name to the list. The criteria he developed for his own fund were not retroactive, and all of Ida's perilous rescues happened before its founding in 1904.

Instead, the altruistic philanthropist gave her money out of his own pocket, in the form of a personal pension of $30 a month. Ida deposited the checks into a savings account for her brother Rud. It was given to him upon her death. And when that unfortunate event occurred, Mrs. Chadwick published a letter that Carnegie had written to her in response to the news that Ida had passed away:

> *Your kind note gives me one source of satisfaction. A happy and favoured man am I to be enabled to help such heroines as Ida Lewis who has passed away. She had no future to fear, having made the best of this life. Fortunate she was in having you as a friend. Let us try to emulate her in the service of our fellows.*

Without any politicking or manipulating, Ida had garnered the support and respect from men such as Carnegie, whom she never met. The year continued to bring good news to the aging keeper.

In 1906 the American Cross of Honor was incorporated by act of Congress. The mission of this service was to select one person each year who rendered the most heroic service in saving lives. In a letter dated October 17, 1907, Ida was notified that she was the person they chose. She was the first American woman to receive this high honor, which included membership in the society and a gold medal complete with certificate. She had been chosen over a multitude of men who had risked their own lives in natural disasters, floods, and large-scale accidents.

This award also dubbed her the bravest woman in the United States. Ida was riding high. While her life had settled into one of a retired celebrity, she enjoyed spending her days as a devout Christian, continuing to care for the island, her brother, and, of course, her beloved light.

⚮

Ida was not destined to live out her days basking in the glory of her past. Her life took a turn for the worse. Changes were in the wind. Along with the rapid-fire societal changes of the Industrial Revolution came a new way of looking at things. Bureaucracy flourished. Systems were put in place under the guise of efficiency. What once was simple had now become complicated. Government became burdened with layers of red tape, and new, younger superiors were ushered in. Formality and distance took the place of the familiar and well-known. And it infiltrated the Lighthouse Bureau.

Perhaps because of her age and the length of time she had tended the light, Ida didn't take well to the changes. Supplies had to be accounted for, and under the new systems, forms were required, often in triplicate. Having to copy something three times must not have made much sense to Ida, who tried her best to comply with the changes. But she made mistakes. And she was curtly reprimanded:

> *Enclosed herewith your Return of Expenditures of oil, wicks and chimneys. You have made an error in subtracting the amount expended for the quarter from the total amount on hand. Correct the same, and return to this office without delay. In the future you will exercise more care in making out this return, as errors made by you delay this office in making its quarterly report to the Lighthouse Board.*

To the woman who had been exalted as both the Grace Darling of America and the darling of the American people, the letter cut deeply. Its impersonal nature was stinging in and of itself; the additional reprimand left a permanent mark. Ida began to worry. For the first time in her life, she questioned her own performance.

The injustice of the missive was appalling. Privately, she searched for the reason behind it. After all, hadn't she effectively tended the light for almost fifty years? There had never been a complaint, not one negative report under her watch. While other lighthouses had been cited for their lack of order, and even their lack of cleanliness (which was considered a high priority to the inspectors), Ida not only had kept impeccable vigilance over the lantern—never once missing even an hour during nightfall—but also had kept a spotless house. The multitude of reporters to the island often made note of her meticulousness. No, there was never a reason for her performance to come under such scrutiny, such criticism. She began to brood and suffer from nervous depression. She had problems sleeping and took to worrying about her aptitude.

Further problems surfaced when she continued to send her usual handwritten notes, requesting supplies and other items, instead of using the appropriate forms. By 1909 the new personnel in the Lighthouse Bureau were beginning to lose patience with what they perceived to be an old lady resisting change:

The reply to your communication of the 27th (February 1909) making requests for 1 barrel of lime, 6 gallons of white paint and 2 gallons of turpentine. You are informed that requisitions for extra supplies at your station should be made on the form provided for that purpose, a copy of which is enclosed.

This type of correspondence continued on and off for the next two years, with each letter digging deeper and deeper into Ida's sense of self-worth, undermining her confidence, and ultimately affecting her health.

By the time she granted a last interview for a full-scale feature piece in *Putnam's Magazine* in February of 1910, she spoke openly of her health: "Rud asked me to help him lift a ladder, and he said, 'You haven't got any more strength than a cat.' I told him I was lifting all I could. But lately I haven't been feeling well—nervous, you know. Maybe it's my heart. I don't know. But then, I'm getting old." The title of the article? "A Half-Forgotten Hero."

Ida had long been one of the Newport attractions. But as she grew older, she grew less tolerant of what was nothing short of rude behavior that was exhibited toward her. In a local newspaper account of September 11, 1909, she exhibited a particular prickliness about her age: "I suppose I am over-sensitive about the age matter, because we all like to remain young as long as we can. But when they tell visitors that I am ninety-eight or one hundred, it is unjust as well as unkind."

Her sensitivity about her age, compounded with criticism from her superiors, only served to make her more susceptible to depression. Feelings of being obsolete and a failure in life soon set in, and things were not about to get better.

In 1910 George Putnam was appointed commissioner of the Lighthouse Board and made sweeping changes in his administration. Lighthouse keepers in general were older like Ida, who was nearing seventy. Putnam set in motion a plan to consolidate lighthouses by grouping them together and having them maintained by one keeper. He also had them auto-mated. Under the new administration, which was meant to bring the system into the twentieth century and to improve efficiency through new regulations, many of the lighthouse keepers had trouble keeping pace. In addition, women were allowed to remain as lighthouse keepers only if they could prove that they could do it solo, without the help of anyone else. Ida was fast becoming outdated.

The next year, on September 29, 1911, Ida received another reprimand from the newly appointed commander of the U.S. Navy, who obviously had little knowledge of Ida Lewis or her renown. After Ida had completed and submitted the lengthy ten-page form known as the Annual Property Return, which accounted for everything in the lighthouse right down to a matchstick, it was promptly returned in the mail, with this note: "Your annual property return is herein returned for correction as you fail to take up the following articles. . . . Unless satisfactory explanation is submitted regarding these discrepancies, the fact will be entered on your record."

Adding insult to injury, Nathan Young, the commander who sent her the letter, didn't even extend the courtesy of signing his name. Its threatening tone implied that Ida had been sloppy in her accounting of supplies and had squandered them.

Its effect was devastating.

Ida was not used to being insulted, and her treatment at the hands of the Lighthouse Bureau was tantamount to just that. For the second and last time, Ida found herself slapped in the face by the master she willingly chose to serve for decades: the federal government.

Chapter 9

IN DEATH, BELOVED

This is home to me and I hope the good Lord will take me away when I have to leave it.

—Ida Lewis

It was the expedition that would test the very steel of a human being, if any man dared undertake it. To early-twentieth-century society, the South Pole was viewed as the final frontier—the only landmass that had yet to be set foot upon, much less explored. Antarctica was known only as a huge patch of icy tundra, barren and cruel. The voyage to the South Pole would prove to be the ultimate survival contest, as it pitted two explorers against each other in a race against time.

The journey would be a constant battle with record snowfalls, blinding blizzards, food deprivation, and frostbite. Knowing all of this, Roald Amundsen (1872–1928), a Norwegian polar explorer, launched his expedition to the South Pole on October 20, 1911. He set out with four men, sleds, and a massive team of dogs. Ten days later, British explorer Robert F. Scott would embark on his own expedition to the South Pole. Amundsen reached Antarctica on December 14, 1911, winning the race to the South Pole. His team spent three days at the pole and then left a Norwegian flag and letters to both the king of Norway and Robert F. Scott before returning.

Perhaps Ida would have identified more with Robert F. Scott, the stalwart British explorer who lost the race to the South Pole but paid the ultimate price in doing so. Scott and his expedition reached the South Pole on January 16, 1912. To Scott's dismay, he found the tent and flag of his competitor, who had arrived more than a month earlier. Their return journey met with disastrous weather, and the entire party perished. Their frozen bodies, along with valuable documents and specimens in their tent, were found eight months later.

One of Scott's last diary entries reveals his valiant spirit: "Had we lived I should have had a tale to tell of the hardihood, endurance, and courage of my companions which would have stirred the heart of every English man. These rough notes and our dead bodies must tell the tale."

And more than halfway around the world, just one day after Amundsen began his journey, faint streaks of orange and pink were crisscrossing the horizon of the Atlantic Ocean. Dawn was breaking on the small island of Lime Rock, as another hero made her way across the hallway to the tiny lantern room just steps from her bedroom. She deftly opened the beveled glass of the sturdy Fresnel lens. She carefully wiped the black carbon that had built up overnight, and checked its clarity. She would later return to the light to make sure that the oil was filled and the lantern readied for its next overnight vigil.

The sum total of Ida's life was encompassed in that flame. "The light is my child, and I know when it needs me, even if I sleep," she said.

It was the child she never had, the center of her small world. It divided her days into a tangible routine, giving her life continuity.

It was a duty from which she drew most, if not all, of her identity. Speaking of the hundreds of boats going in and out of the harbor, she once said, "It's part of my happiness to know they are depending on me to guide them safely."

The flame dictated her life. It ruled her time, but she drew great comfort in knowing that it gave her life purpose. Even though the world hailed her for saving the lives of eighteen people, Ida had a greater motivation. It was out there beyond the faintest rays of her light. It was the collage of all those she saved because she kept the light and provided a beacon of safety to the faceless mariners, the nameless ships, and the unknown schooners. It was for them that she kept the light. It was for the countless numbers she would never know, those she would never row out to rescue in the face of gale winds, those for whom she would never risk her own life, those who would never taste a hot molasses toddy. It was for those who were doing their job well, just as she was doing hers.

She was their mistress, with the sole charge of keeping them out of harm's way. It was the mere existence of the light that saved those unnumbered sailors every night. And it was she, Ida Lewis, who had the weighty mission to keep it burning. There must have been thousands upon thousands whom the light had saved with her faithful assistance. So many the world would never know because their names would not be etched in newsprint, or uttered on the lips of society, or recounted by children searching for a hero to worship.

Ida extinguished the flame on October 21, 1911, for what would be her last time.

She crossed the hallway and dressed for the day. She made her way downstairs to bring in a bundle of wood from outside to stoke the fire in the kitchen and to make breakfast for her brother Rud. Carrying the armload of wood, Ida collapsed to the floor. Wood tumbled around her. She suffered a massive stroke, at the time commonly known as apoplexy.

Her brother awoke at 7:30 a.m., surprised and somewhat dismayed that his sister had let him oversleep, and wondered where she was. He wandered from room to room calling for her. He found her lying on the floor of the kitchen in front of the hearth, logs all about her. He rushed to her and listened to her chest. She was still alive, and after trying to bring her back to consciousness, Rud succeeded in reviving her. Ida asked him to call for their doctor and then slipped back into unconsciousness. She would never speak again. Rud had to leave his sister unattended to row to shore to find the doctor and bring him back to the island. He was sick at the prospect that she might be dead upon their return.

"She was semi-conscious," he later told the *Newport Daily News*. "I did what I could for her, but as I knew aid had to be summoned. I was forced to leave her alone while I rowed ashore. . . . When I returned to the lighthouse, my sister had grown much worse and had lost all consciousness."

The following three days marked a deathwatch in the local newspapers, and the story was picked up by newspapers as far away as Europe. Ida was popular all over again. Although she had receded subtly into the background of society's fickle tapestry of celebrity, she never left its heart as the Grace Darling of America.

Upon hearing of Ida's condition, the War Department sent a notice requesting that the artillery practice at Fort Adams be suspended in deference to her condition, as those attending her sent word that the loud shelling seemed to agitate her.

Hundreds of telegrams arrived from both the distinguished and the unknown, wishing her a return to good health. After reading the news of Ida's stroke, Elsie Vanderbilt left her home in Tuxedo, New York, early the next day to travel to Harbourview. She was rowed out to the island and spent a few final hours with the unconscious heroine, her friend.

Ida remained in a deep coma until shortly before 8:00 a.m. on Tuesday, October 24, 1911. It was then that Idawalley Zoradia Lewis Wilson surrendered to a quiet death at the age of sixty-nine. At her side were her brother Rud, her doctor, and several close family friends, including Amelia Shaw Kerr, who would handle all the funeral arrangements and the viewing of the body.

In the minds of those who knew her well—especially her brother, who was quite outspoken to the local press—there was no question about why she died so suddenly. Her stroke, they said, was due to stress, as well as the nervous depression brought about by ongoing changes in the Lighthouse Department and the formal reprimands Ida had received.

Being chided was not easy for Ida to stomach, especially since she had a meticulous sense of duty and no doubt had grown used to being highly valued. She was also a historical figure who had the uncommon vantage point of watching herself become a legend in her own lifetime.

So it was no surprise when exaggerated and inflammatory reports appeared in the local newspapers. The *Newport Daily News* ran a subhead directly under her obituary headline that read, "Fatal Illness Probably Due to Worry over Department Reports."

Adding more fuel to the fire was a rumored report circulating just days before she collapsed. According to the October 19, 1911, issue of the *Newport Daily News,* new plans were under discussion to reconfigure the buoying and navigational aids in Narragansett Bay. The piece strongly suggested that Lime Rock Light was under scrutiny and that it quite possibly might be abolished altogether and Ida removed as its keeper. The newspaper also ran a photograph of Ida along with the story, which ended on a somewhat dour yet hopeful note, referring to the gold medal Ida had received from Congress years before: "It is suggested that in view of what Congress did in regard to Ida Lewis that body may take a hand if it is proposed to abolish her lighthouse."

In fact, on the day before her death, the newspaper sent a telegram to the lighthouse inspector, with the single line: "Is Lime Rock Light to be abandoned?" The response: "No information to that effect at this time."

Upon reading the story, or at least hearing of its content, Ida, who had already been deeply questioning her competency and suffering great consternation over the lighthouse inspector's curt treatment, had fallen into dark despair. Ida had once said, "This is home to me and I hope the good Lord will take me away when I have to leave it." In light of the rumored decommissioning, her words were eerily prophetic.

Her wish was granted. That day, the steamship *Priscilla* from the Fall River Line plaintively tolled its bell as it steamed past Lime Rock, in honor and tribute to its former mistress.

The sea was inordinately mild, or as the *Newport Daily News* recounted, "as calm as a millpond and the last water voyage was made under the most pleasant conditions." Ida's body made its last trip across the familiar route from Lime Rock to Wellington Avenue in downtown Newport on the morning of October 27. She was accompanied by the undertaker and harbormaster on that final trip.

Her brother Rud stood stoically on the rocks of their island home and watched as the body of his dead sister left the island for the last time. He said, "That is the way poor Ida wanted to leave the light when she left for good, in her casket."

A large number of people gathered on the shore as her body was removed from the transport boat and taken to Thames Street Episcopal Methodist Church, where she lay in state from 10:00 a.m. to 2:00 p.m. The casket was open, draped with a silver broadcloth decorated with column corners and surrounded by an abundance of large floral arrangements. A single arrangement given by the Sorosis Society of New York was placed on the closed end of the casket, and a simple silver plate bore the inscription:

IDA LEWIS
DIED OCTOBER 24, 1911
AGED 69 YEARS

Throngs of people streamed by her coffin to take a last view of this contemporary heroine. One report estimated that some 1,439 visitors paid their respects. The *Newport Daily News* reported:

> *They saw a peaceful face, a little thinner perhaps than many remembered, but without any suffering. The hands, thin and showing her age and work more than the calm features, were crossed over her breast. They were the hands of one who had worked, strong hands which seemed able to do the task they were called upon to perform with the oars and which had proved this for so many long years and under so many varying conditions.*

Dignitaries flocked to the service as well, the government being represented by Admiral R. P. Rodgers and Rear Admiral French E. Chadwick. Other mourners included fellow keepers, mariners, a flock of men from the lifesaving station located in Newport, as well as a number of prominent wealthy Newporters, cottagers, and local residents.

Appropriately, Fort Adams played a prominent role in the funeral proceedings. Six soldiers from the encampment acted as pallbearers, and the Fort Adams band played select hymns during the service, as well as afterward during the processional to the gravesite.

The Reverend Stanley C. Hughes, rector of Trinity, spoke of the dead heroine as being "the most remarkable woman Newport ever produced."

Then the Reverend W. F. Geisler, pastor of the church, rose from his seat and captivated the public with his stirring eulogy:

Let no one think that Ida Lewis can be buried. Her worn-out form may be placed beneath the clods, but still will there come the traveler from near or from far to look upon her grave. . . . To him, will she still be alive and so will be with us. We will tell our children, and our children will tell their children the tale of the rescues of this lighthouse keeper in the harbor of Newport. She achieved immortality.

The life of this unique woman is its own best eulogy. She herself opened the door and was welcomed into that high society, the aristocracy of heroism, the great of heart. To her the need was the duty, the cost was never counted. There were no terrors to her of wind or wave or rock or freezing cold. The cry of distress alone struck fear and courage and action into being and when even the light did not avail to warm and guide, she went down into the waters, among its perils, to the rescue, as if it were an ordinary task.

He continued to extol her courageous heart:

This was not, however, the work of flesh and blood, of nerve and muscle alone. The strength and steadiness of muscle and nerve—a strength and steadiness born of simple temperate life—were indeed requisite to her. Heroic efforts and yet they would have been soft untwisted flax without a great spirit and a will of steel. To this spirit, the heart of this wonderful woman, we bow today and do honor unto ourselves. As the light that she kept so faithfully was a beacon to the mariner with the circle of its reach, so the light of her brave unselfish spirit became an inspiration of courage to the whole world, the fame of her deeds having filled it. She who seldom went beyond the limits of her native city, became a citizen of the world—her name, a household treasure because she kept the light shining and feared not the duty perilous.

The spillover from the attendance in the packed church filled the street outside, at least seventy-five yards in either direction. Carriages lined the streets, and a large number of cottagers were in attendance. Mourners lined the route from the church to the cemetery, where the body was interred following an elaborate funeral procession, which included two carriages overflowing with floral arrangements and six soldiers solemnly carrying the casket.

In honor of her passing, stores in the business district shut down, and flags were voluntarily and ceremoniously kept at half-staff on public buildings, such as the customs office, public schools, and city hall, and on most ships in the harbor. The bells in the harbor rang in unison to honor her passing.

Ida's body was committed to the ground that afternoon, placed in a burial site next to the graves of her father, mother, and sister in what was called Old Cemetery, or the Common-ground, on Farewell Street in Newport. Her epitaph read: THE GRACE DARLING OF AMERICA, KEEPER OF LIME ROCK LIGHTHOUSE, NEWPORT HARBOR.

So ended the life of Ida Lewis. It was not necessarily a happy one and never could be characterized as carefree. She spent most of it caring for others, performing mundane, backbreaking tasks, and watching over the light at Lime Rock. But it was a life she herself chose. If anything, she fought to retain her simple world in spite of her early notoriety. Even though she remained unchanged and untainted by the attention society gave her, part of her must have identified with the title "Heroine of Lime Rock." Above her bed hung a framed picture of Grace Darling's gravesite. Perhaps in some corner of her heart, she did view herself as the American Grace Darling. Maybe that connection to Grace inspired her to live up to the expectation the world had placed before her. She never did want fame, and she never reaped much from it. And she never once ventured a foot on the path to which fame could have led.

IDA LEWIS LIGHTHOUSE

Our good deeds, although registered in heaven, are by our fellow sinners but too often buried with our bones.

—COLONEL GEORGE BREWERTON, BIOGRAPHER OF IDA LEWIS

The light of Lime Rock passed out of the hands of the Lewis family for the first and last time several weeks after Ida's death. Her brother Rud took over as interim lighthouse keeper the day she died. He had sent a correspondence to the inspector of the Third District the day before she actually died. Knowing the end was near for his dear sister, Rud informed the man that he was prepared to continue tending the light, because of his sister's condition:

> *Now unconscious due to a severe stroke of apoplexy . . . her condition is critical. I have accordingly taken charge here since then, since I have lived with her in cooperation for nearly 25 years. Until the course of conditions change, one way or the other, I presume I am expected to continue in this capacity.*

He had barely sent the telegram when he had to send another, notifying the Bureau of Lighthouses of his sister's death. He received a telegram in reply from the inspector:

Your telegram has just been received. This office desires to express sympathy and regret for the death of your sister, Mrs. Ida Lewis Wilson, former keeper. If you will continue to care for the light until a new keeper can be sent to relieve you, your kindness will be appreciated.

Even if asked to take over the position, Rud was so distraught over Ida's passing that he found being alone on the island unbearable. He left the island two weeks later. Evard Jansen was appointed for $516 a year (compared to the $750 Ida had been making at the time of her death). Jansen had been a lighthouse keeper at Sandy Hook in New Jersey, following a lifetime of service in both the army and the navy. He remained on Lime Rock until it was deactivated in 1927. He and his wife had a baby girl while on the island, whom they named Ida Lewis Jansen.

Rud, having no family members except three half-nieces who were born to his half-brother Joseph in Massachusetts, moved off Lime Rock after living there most of his life. He moved in with family friends, Mr. and Mrs. Edgar Kerr, in the seaport area of downtown Newport. He died of a cerebral hemorrhage at Newport Hospital on November 9, 1917, almost six years to the day that he left Lime Rock.

Ida did not leave a will but had made it known that she wanted all of her valuables and memorabilia left to the Newport Historical Society. For most of the latter part of her life, she had shared her personal belongings with her brother Rud, and he inherited them. The pension so kindly transmitted to her from Andrew Carnegie was transferred to her brother.

Barely two months after Ida's death, a movement to change the name of Lime Rock Lighthouse to Ida Lewis Lighthouse was launched. The desires of local Newporters apparently fell on deaf ears at the Bureau of Lighthouses.

On November 15, 1911, shortly after Ida's death, Horatio Wood of Newport sent off a letter to his U.S. senator, George Peabody Wetmore, who was abroad at the time. Wood was a member of the Cadets of Temperance and a staunch supporter of Ida Lewis. When Wetmore returned a month later, he sent a copy of the letter along with his own note to George Putnam, the commissioner of the Bureau of Lighthouses. The response came within five days, stating that "lighthouses and other aids to navigation are without exception named according to their geographical position, and any departure from this system or change in the name of an aid when not essential, would in the opinion of the Bureau be undesirable, as liable to be confusing or dangerous to mariners."

It is not known whether Ida's fears about the rumored decommissioning were grounded in truth. In his correspondence to Senator Wetmore, Commissioner Putnam made reference to the decommissioning, the rumors of which had obviously reached him (even newspapers with wide circulation reprinted the theory that Ida's stroke was brought on by concerns about the lighthouse and her own performance).

"I beg to state that it is not contemplated, so far as the Bureau is informed, that this light shall be discontinued, and its discontinuance has not been considered," Putnam stated.

The letter from Putnam seemed to suffice for Senator Wetmore and presumably Mr. Wood and the others backing the idea. The issue of renaming Lime Rock in honor of Ida Lewis seemed to have been by and large forgotten.

More than a decade later, the correspondences resumed between members of the General Assembly of Rhode Island and the Bureau of Lighthouses. And this time, the result would be dramatically different.

The first letter appears in early 1923, written by Clark Burdick, U.S. representative for the First District in Rhode Island, asking the bureau to investigate reasons why the lighthouse could not have its name changed. Unlike his counterpart in the Senate more than a decade earlier, Burdick took on the mission with a plan. Burdick—the point man for a local movement in Newport, where varying groups were circulating a petition among Newporters, the gentry, and the working class—had tremendous grassroots support. And he didn't take no for an answer.

It's not clear what prompted the movement to be resurrected, or why it should crop up so many years after Ida's death. Perhaps it was because the townspeople and Rhode Islanders in general had taken to calling Lime Rock the Ida Lewis Light. Lime Rock had been completely abandoned as its name. Whatever the reasoning, Burdick took up the torch for the swelling throng of Newporters who had circulated a petition to have the name formally changed.

In a brief letter in response to Burdick's request for information, which the Bureau of Lighthouses hoped would close the matter once and for all, Putnam once again stated that "regulations for governing the Lighthouse Service do not permit complying with your request." But Burdick was persistent, asking for the specifics of the so-called regulations, and he waited patiently for a month while the bureau stalled. Finally a letter arrived in May, in which Putnam made little effort to veil his elation: "I take pleasure in quoting you the following extract from the Regulations of Lighthouse Service 1918."

He quoted: "The name recommended for an aid shall, when practicable, include the name of the locality to be marked, and in that case should be taken from the most recent charts of the United States Coast and Geodetic Survey."

Burdick now knew that his initial correspondence with the Bureau of Lighthouses was as futile as Wetmore's earlier request had been. The same administration was in place, and he received the same reply about navigational safety being tied to the geographic naming of each lighthouse. Acknowledging receipt of Putnam's letter, Burdick said he understood that the bureau could not take favorable action on the name change because of the cited regulations. However, he continued:

> In your first letter, it was spoken of as a universal rule, and I presumed that perhaps it was unwritten law, or precedent, which can be broken. An instance of this is when Ida Lewis was appointed a keeper, when no woman had ever before so appointed, as I understand it.

Then he cleverly asked that Putnam send him a copy of the regulations so that he could turn it over to his friends who advocated the change.

Whether Putnam did this is unknown. What is known is that Burdick decided to go to the source: the U.S. Coast and Geodetic Survey, which was responsible for the nuts-and-bolts surveying of properties and had been cited by Putnam as the deciding body for the names of lighthouses. His thinking was acute. In December 1923, Burdick sent off a letter outlining his proposal for the name change: "I presume that your Bureau, with the authority vested in it for compiling charts, can recommend a change in name in such an instance as this."

If the U.S. Coast and Geodetic Survey could come up with no good reasons for not renaming the island, and he could get them to agree with his position, it would add more political pressure to the Bureau of Lighthouses, and specifically Commissioner Putnam, to reverse the decision.

During this time, more and more organizations, including the Sons of Temperance, private citizens, mariners, and the like, added their names to the growing petition, adding momentum to what was becoming a full-scale movement across the state of Rhode Island.

What may have been fueling Putnam's opposition to the name change was hinted at in a letter from the first assistant superintendent, the lighthouse inspector for the district in which Lime Rock was stationed. In correspondence to the commissioner, he urged that any change might interfere with the decisions that were already being made regarding Lime Rock. He said that the lighthouse "is of practically no use, and it is the intention of this office, as soon as funds will permit, to do away with the present light structure, and establish in its place an unwatched acetylene light." If the name was changed to Ida Lewis Lighthouse, the concern was that people would be up in arms over its discontinuance.

It was all a moot point, for in less than a month, the Coast and Geodetic Survey came back with its reply. The officials fully and enthusiastically endorsed the idea. At its monthly meeting in February, it approved the name change, with the provision that the Lighthouse Bureau agreed. A letter was sent to Putnam, encouraging his bureau's endorsement.

In conjunction with the approval of the Coast and Geodetic Survey, the Rhode Island General Assembly passed a resolution favoring the change, as did the City of Newport. At the time, the *Providence Journal* came out with a lengthy article about the movement to change the name of the lighthouse. The article detailed the life story of Rhode Island's heroine and drew further public support for the movement.

Defeated, Putnam gave in, and in 1924 the bureau gave its approval to the name change, being the first and only time such an honor was paid to a lighthouse keeper.

Automatic lights were fast replacing the lanterns of a bygone lighthouse era. The new acetylene lights did not have to be maintained like the old ones, and given the new lighthouse on Goat Island and other navigational aids, the Ida Lewis Lighthouse was no longer practicable as a navigational aid to mariners.

The lighthouse was deactivated in 1927, three years after its renaming.

Jansen and his wife and child left the island house when the new tower with the automated light was erected. The house fell into disrepair. Townspeople watched as the paint began to chip away from the brick edifice. The shuttered windows broke open from the whipping wind from the sea, and the doors banged. What once was the neatly kept home of their beloved heroine was falling apart.

Dr. Horace Beck, a leading Newporter, couldn't bear to see the neglect of the lighthouse and the possibility that it would be lost to history if destroyed. According to his wife, who recalled the series of events that saved the lighthouse many years later, Beck and philanthropist Arthur Curtiss James jointly decided to buy the lighthouse from the government. As only a small part of the island was actually being used by the government (for the skeleton tower for the automated light), the sale was readily agreed to. Mrs. Beck recalled the action:

When Ida Lewis Light was decommissioned, it was put up for sale in New York. Dr. Beck heard of it the day before it was to be auctioned off and it was said that the fishermen were going to buy it for a place to sort their catch, the discard of course to be thrown overboard. When Dr. Beck came home for dinner that evening, he remarked what a splendid yacht club it would make. In talking it over, I suggested he get in touch with Mr. Arthur Curtiss James. He telephoned Mr. James who concurred with the yacht club and said to get down there and buy it, and how much to pay. Time was short but we reached Newport Long Wharf just in time as the New York boat's gangplank was being pulled in. The captain was an old friend, saw him and had the gangplank put back. At the auction, Dr. Beck realized that the fishermen were determined to have the place and that the price would be in excess of what Mr. James had mentioned. Luckily, Mr. James was reached by telephone and his succinct answer was, "You want to buy it, don't you?"

In 1928 the newly formed Narragansett Bay Regatta Association bought the lighthouse and most of the island for $7,200, to preserve its history and create a perfect site for a yacht club in desirable Bretton Cove. Later that year, the Ida Lewis Yacht Club was officially organized, and it was listed among Newport's clubs for the first time in 1929. Ceremoniously, on July 4, 1929, a full sixty years to the day that Newport celebrated Ida Lewis Day, the Ida Lewis Yacht Club opened its doors. Its flag is a small lighthouse encircled by eighteen stars, one for each of her rescues. (The official total varies from eighteen to twenty-five, depending on sources.) The first commodore was, appropriately, Arthur Curtiss James, and his beautiful yacht *Aloha* became the honorary flagship. Charter members of the Ida Lewis Yacht Club included descendants of the Newport elite, including the Astors and the Vanderbilts.

Arthur Curtiss James had a wooden walkway built to the rock, and the house was renovated and turned into a clubhouse. Floats and ramps were added. Several rooms of the house were restored to the time when Ida lived there and tended light. Housed in the old light tower is a replica light. The original lantern is now on display at the Newport Historical Society Museum. The club currently has 375 members, many of whom moor their boats in Bretton Cove.

At the opening ceremony, Commodore James spoke of his feeling for the future of the club, as his large yacht was the lone vessel sitting in the harbor. According to the July 5, 1929, *Evening News,* he said:

My chief ambition for this yacht club is the revival of small boating. As a boy I lived in Newport. There were hundreds of small sailing vessels and frequent races were held. This interest in boating diminished as I grew up. I am anxious to bring back those days.

His wish has been granted. Newport is synonymous with boating, and on a clear summer day, as far as the eye can see, the horizon around the Ida Lewis Yacht Club is dotted with seafaring vessels.

Ida's name is also tied to the U.S. Junior Women's Double-handed Championship for the Ida Lewis Trophy, which began in 1995 and is a U.S. Sailing national championship event held at rotating locations around the country. The participants must be female sailors between the ages of thirteen and eighteen. The winners have their names inscribed on the Ida Lewis Trophy, which is housed at the Ida Lewis Yacht Club. While Ida never sailed, the championship honors her youth and athleticism.

In 1963 the Coast Guard, which had taken over the Lighthouse Service in 1939, deactivated the light altogether. The yacht club later received special permission to put a light back in the old lantern casing. It is still lit today as a private aid to navigation.

In a special honor to lighthouse keepers, the U.S. Coast Guard came out with a new class of boats: the Keeper Class coastal buoy tender. Honoring those who tended America's lighthouses, the cutters are named after keepers. The first vessel of this class was christened *Ida Lewis*. The *Ida Lewis* is docked in Newport and is a state-of-the-art, 175-foot vessel that takes daily and overnight trips around coastal Rhode Island to check the positions of buoys and maintain them. In 2001 the U.S. Coast Guard also dedicated a training center to Ida Lewis in Cape May, New Jersey.

The men of the cutter *Ida Lewis* were granted permission by the city council to refurbish Ida Lewis's gravestone, which had fallen into disrepair. The new monument features four-foot granite pillars shaped like lighthouses. A steel chain connects the pillars.

The U.S. Coast Guard continues to honor the past while attending the tradition of seeing mariners safely through the night and the storm.

It is a mission that is carried out in the spirit of Ida Lewis.

AFTERWORD

In the writing of this book, I found that several myths about Ida Lewis needed to be clarified.

Carnegie Hero Trust Fund: Many accounts of her life contain the persistent, mistaken notion that Ida Lewis was a recipient of the Carnegie Hero Trust Fund, now the Carnegie Hero Commission, based in Pittsburgh, Pennsylvania. According to the commission's historian, there is no record of Ida Lewis Wilson ever being an awardee of a medal or of a pension, as has been reported in other accounts. The fund was started in 1904 by Andrew Carnegie and honors those who risk their lives in saving others.

But what I did find and included in this text was newspaper documentation verifying that because Carnegie could not go back on the rules of his own commission and give her the honor retroactively, he could do it himself, independent of the commission. Apparently he compensated Ida monthly out of his own pocket, to ensure that she was taken care of in her old age.

Marriage: According to quoted accounts by her brother Rudolph, Ida and her husband lived together for two years before she returned home. Other sources claim that the marriage lasted only several months. Because she had not officially been appointed as lighthouse keeper, it is impossible to verify the length of time she was away. No letters or notes exchanged between Ida and her family during the period she was away have survived to the present day.

Opinions differ as to whether Ida Lewis and her husband first took up residence in Newport or in Connecticut. Since an overwhelming number of accounts state that they were married for several years (taking *several* to mean "two"), they would have been married from October 23, 1870, to at least late 1872. Although an exhaustive search through Bridgeport city records and newspaper accounts unearthed very little regarding this matter, an entry for William H. Wilson, listing him as a "seaman" who owned a house in Black Rock, appears out of the blue in the Bridgeport City Directory for the year spanning 1872–1873. If the names were collected during the year prior to printing, that would mean he was living there in late 1871. This places him within the time frame of his conjugal marriage to Ida, whose name would not necessarily appear next to his as she was not the owner of the house. It is a deduction, but I believe it is a reasonable one.

Death: According to most newspaper accounts, Ida Lewis died of apoplexy, or stroke, which occurred on the morning of October 21, 1911. She lingered and finally passed away three days later. Her vital statistics concur that it was a stroke that killed her. While *Notable American Women* (1607–1950) accounts for her death differently, saying she died from a cerebral hemorrhage, "stroke syndrome" includes cerebral hemorrhaging, according to *Dorland's Medical Dictionary.*

There is also some discrepancy in the dates, according to different tertiary sources, regarding the deaths of family members. Death and marriage records found at Newport City Hall were used in this book as the source of these dates and information about her relatives.

Rescues: There is some confusion about the second rescue. According to Brewerton, three soldiers were in the skiff, and two jumped overboard. Other accounts, including *Putnam's Magazine,* place the number at two, with one of them being a soldier, the other being a young boy whom he had hired to row him home. This could be a confusion between two rescues, or just simply wrong. Given that Ida herself sanctioned the writing of the Brewerton booklet and other accounts concur, his account of the incident was the one used here.

Appointment: It has been passed down through several generations that Ida Lewis was the first woman appointed a lighthouse keeper. A lot would depend on the definition of the word *appointment.* This changed over time; appointments were originally made by the president and later were made by the secretary of the Treasury. As far as I could discern, other women were appointed as keepers, perhaps not with the formal letter and hefty annual salary that Ida received, but they were appointed nonetheless.

BIBLIOGRAPHY

Although many sources were investigated, not all possible sources have been used. The following books, newspaper articles, and reports were used in compiling this book.

Adamson, Hans Christian. *Keepers of the Lights.* New York: Greenberg, 1955.

Annual Report of the Commissioner of Lighthouses to the Secretary of Commerce and Labor for the Fiscal Year Ended June 1911. Washington, D.C.: U.S. Government Printing Office, 1911.

Annual Report of the Light-House Board to the Treasury for the Year 1868. Washington, D.C.: U.S. Government Printing Office, 1868.

Annual Report of the Secretary of the Treasury on the State of the Finances for the Fiscal Year Ended June 30, 1939. Washington, D.C.: U.S. Government Printing Office, 1939.

Auchincloss, Louis. *The Vanderbilt Era: Profiles of a Gilded Age.* New York: Charles Scribner's Sons, 1989.

Bachand, Robert. *Northeast Lights: Lighthouses and Lightships (Rhode Island to Cape May, NJ).* Norwalk, Conn.: Sea Sports Publications, 1989.

Basler, Roy P., ed. *The Collected Works of Abraham Lincoln.* www.abrahamlincolnonline.org.

Bassett, John Spencer. *A Short History of the United States.* New York: Macmillan, 1927.

Beard, Charles A., and Mary R. Beard. *The Rise of American Civilization.* New York: Macmillan, 1927.

Boddington, Captain Jack. "The Life Saving Benevolent Association of New York and Its Medals." *The Journals of the Orders and Medals Research Society* 24, no. 3, Autumn 1985.

Brewerton, Colonel George. A. *Ida Lewis, the Heroine of Lime Rock.* 1869.

Carruth, Gorton and Associates. *American Facts & Dates.* New York: Thomas Y. Crowell, 1956.

Cherry-Garrard, Apsley G. B. *The Worst Journey in the World: Antarctic, 1910–1913.* New York: Lincoln MacVeagh/ Dial Press, 1930.

Clauson, J. E. "A Half-Forgotten Heroine." *Putnam's Magazine,* February 1910.

Clifford, Mary Louise, and J. Candace Clifford. *Women Who Kept the Light: An Illustrated History of Female Lighthouse Keepers.* Williamsburg, Va.: Cypress Communications, 1993.

Conway, John S. *The United States Lighthouse Service 1923.* Washington, D.C.: U.S. Government Printing Office, 1923.

Curti, Merle. *The Growth of American Thought.* New York: Harper and Brothers, 1943.

Encyclopedia Americana. New York and Chicago: Americana Company, 1948.

The Evening News, July 5, 1929.

Frank Leslie's Illustrated Newspaper, August 1869.

Hamm, William A. *The American People.* D. C. Heath, 1939.

Harper's New Monthly Magazine, April 15, 1869.

Harper's Weekly, July 31, 1869.

Hicks, John D. *The American Nation.* New York: Houghton Mifflin, 1941.

Hockett, Homer C. *Political and Social History of the United States (1492–1828).* New York: Macmillan, 1925.

Holland, Francis Ross, Jr. *America's Lighthouses: Their Illustrated History since 1716.* Brattleboro, Vt.: Stephen Greene Press, 1972.

James, Edward T., ed. *Notable American Women: A Biographical Dictionary,* vol. II, G–O (1607–1950). Cambridge, Mass.: Belknap Press of Harvard University Press, 1971.

Johnson, Arnold Burges. *The Modern Light-House Service.* Washington, D.C.: U.S. Government Printing Office, 1890.

The Journal of the U.S. Life-Saving Service Heritage Association, no. 12, Fall 1999.

Keeper's Log, Fall 1986.

Ladies' Home Journal, "Ida Lewis at Home," July 1890.

MacDowell, Dorothy Kelley. *Commodore Vanderbilt and His Family: A Biographical Account of the Descendants of Cornelius and Sophia Johnson Vanderbilt.* New York: D. K. MacDowell, 1989.

Marcus, Jon, and Susan Cole Kelly. *Lighthouses of New England.* Stilwater, Minn.: Voyageur Press, 2001.

McCullough, David. *The Great Bridge.* New York: Simon and Schuster, 1972.

Mitford, Jessica. *Grace Had an English Heart.* New York: E. P. Dutton, 1989.

Morison, Samuel Eliot, and Henry Steele Commager. *The Growth of the American Republic (1000–1865).* New York: Oxford University Press, 1942.

———. *The Growth of the American Republic (1865–1942).* New York: Oxford University Press, 1942.

Muzzey, David. *The United States of America—From the Civil War.* Boston: Ginn & Co., 1924.

Nettels, Curtis Putnam. *Roots of American Civilization.* New York: F S Crofts and Company, 1938.

Nevins, Allan. *A Brief History of the United States.* New York: Oxford University Press, 1942.

———. *Ordeal of the Union.* New York: Charles Scribner's Sons, 1947.

Nevins, Allan, and Henry Steele Commager. *A Short History of the United States*. New York: Random House, 1943.

The New International Year Book, 1946. New York and London: Funk and Wagnalls, 1946.

Newport Daily News, various clips from August 5, 1869, to October 29, 1969.

Newport Herald, October 28, 1911; various clips from July 5, 1869, to October 16, 1911.

Newport History: The Bulletin of the Newport Historical Society 61 and 62, nos. 209–216.

New York Herald Tribune, April 15, 1869.

New York Times, October 25, 1911; October 27, 1911; October 29, 1911.

New York World, October 31, 1932.

Oceans (published by Oceanic Society), November 1985.

Patterson, Jerry E. *The Vanderbilts*. New York: Harry N. Abrams, 1989.

The Providence Sunday Journal, February 17, 1924.

Putnam, George R. *Lighthouses and Lightships of the United States*. Boston: Houghton Mifflin, 1933.

Putnam's Magazine, February 1910.

A Record of Newport Deaths, vol. 5, 82, 194; vol. 7, 120.

A Record of Newport Marriages, vol. 1, 129.

Revolution, July 15, 1869, 26; September 2, 1869, 129–130.

Schlesinger, Arthur Meier. *Political and Social Growth of the United States, 1852–1933.* New York: Macmillan, 1939.

Smith, Darrell Hevenor, and Fred Wilbur Powell. *The Coast Guard: Its History, Activities, and Organization.* Washington, D.C.: Brookings Institution, 1929.

Snow, Edward Rowe. *Famous Lighthouses of America.* New York: Dodd, Mead, 1955.

———. *Famous Lighthouses of New England.* Yankee Publishing, 1945.

Twenty-fourth Annual Report of the U.S. Department of Commerce 1936. Washington, D.C.: U.S. Government Printing Office, 1936.

U.S. Coast Guard. *Historically Famous Lighthouses.* Washington, D.C.: Public Information Division, U.S. Coast Guard, 1972.

Weiss, George. *The Service: Its History, Activities, and Organization.* Baltimore, Md.: The Johns Hopkins Press, 1926.

Wright, Louis B. *The Atlantic Frontier.* New York: Alfred A. Knopf, 1947.

INDEX

ABOUT THE AUTHOR

Lenore Skomal is the author of fourteen books, including *Lady Liberty: The History of the Statue of Liberty*. When her story about Ida Lewis was first released under the title *The Keeper of Lime Rock: The Remarkable True Story of Ida Lewis, America's Most Celebrated Lighthouse Keeper* (Running Press, 2002), it won prestigious honors from the New York Public Library and accolades from *Publisher's Weekly* and *Booksense*. Her weekly humor column and videocast (www.goerie .com) has won numerous Society of Professional Journalists awards. Skomal has also taught journalism and creative writing at the college level.